Acting Edition

CW01497698

The Keen Collection Volume 11

The Doctor Will See You Shortly
by Laura Neill

The Odds Are...
by Dennis A. Allen II

Milewalkers
by Jesús I. Valles

SAMUEL FRENCH

ISBN 978-0-573-71152-7

www.concordtheatricals.com
www.concordtheatricals.co.uk

TABLE OF CONTENTS

ABOUT KEEN TEENS

Founded in 2000, Keen Company is an award-winning Off-Broadway theatre producing stories that celebrate the complexities of hope and the joys of the human condition. Central to Keen Company's mission is to present theatre that patrons can identify with and connect to. The Keen Teens program is the cornerstone of the company's outreach and educational efforts, bringing the company's values to the high school stage by developing new work tailored specifically to teen actors and audiences. When first creating Keen Teens in 2007, the company found that teachers did not have access to material intended for a high school stage. Educators were left to present either classic plays never designed for teen actors, or material created specifically for school groups that lacked richness or relevance. Through Keen Teens, the company began commissioning original plays and musicals that are as complex and multilayered as the lives of high school students today, penned by accomplished professional playwrights and musical theatre writers.

There are two components to Keen Teens: The first is a free program for New York City-area high school students to work alongside professional writers, directors, and designers to rehearse and premiere these plays Off-Broadway. The second is that the plays then go on to be published and licensed through our partners at Concord Theatricals as *The Keen Collection*.

The Keen Collection is made up of comedies, dramas, and musicals; scripts range from the sincere to the absurd, from the existential to the most intimate. Some deal head-on with topical issues, others simply aim to provide smart, contemporary material. These original pieces have been created by many of the most talented writers working today, including Bekah Brunstetter, Kristoffer Diaz, Madeleine George, C.A. Johnson, Greg Kotis, Mike Lew, James Tyler, Leah Nanako Winkler, and Lauren Yee. This group includes finalists for the Pulitzer, Wendy Wasserstein, and Susan Smith Blackburn Prizes; and winners of the Yale Drama Series Prize, Horton Foote Playwriting Award, and more. Their theatrical work has been produced professionally on and Off-Broadway, and their writing has reached an international audience on TV shows including *Billions, Elsbeth, Girls, GLOW, Mad Men, Severance, Somebody Somewhere, Tales of the City,* and *This Is Us.*

As well as being tailored to the social and emotional world of teens, these plays are also designed to be accessible in educational settings. All scripts run thirty minutes, with simple design elements, large ensembles, and flexible casting requirements. Each play can be presented on its own or in combination with other *Keen Collection* titles on a shared bill.

Keen Teens has made possible the Off-Broadway debut of over three hundred young actors and has led to the publication of over thirty-five new one-act plays and musicals, which are regularly produced not only in the United States, but in countries around the world, from Australia to Singapore.

For more information, please visit www.keencompany.org/keenteens.

KEEN TEENS AMBASSADORS

Keen Teens is made possible with the support of our Keen Teens Ambassadors:

The Doctor Will See You Shortly

by Laura Neill

THE DOCTOR WILL SEE YOU SHORTLY premiered with Keen Company (Jonathan Silverstein, Artistic Director) as part of the Keen Teens Festival of New Work at Theatre Row in New York City on May 17, 2024. The performance was directed by Susanna Jaramillo, with sets by Yi-Hsuan (Ant) Ma and Yun Yen, costumes by Dan Wang, lights by Hayley Garcia Parnell, sound by Eden Segbefia, and props by Caitlyn Murphy. The Production Stage Manager was Sloane Fischer. The cast was as follows:

MARI .... Kiesse Yengo-Passy

ZAZ ....Juliet Burns

BROOK ....Zoya Szasz

CHARLIE...................................... Samiya Williams

AJ .... Zosia Sinton

ELLA..Bianca Vigilante

SERENA..Yngrid Jimenez

DOC...Annahlyn Barrett

FAY .... Victoria Caraballosa

BABY ....Madisyn Martin

ENSEMBLE................................. Ida Footman Beckett,
Red Permaul, Alicia Seetaram

CHARACTERS

PATIENTS

MARI – Edgy goth nerd. Diagnosed with anxiety. Has anxiety, and undiagnosed endometriosis.

ZAZ – Soccer jock. Diagnosed with nothing; awaiting test results for STDs. Has herpes. Also has ovarian cysts, which frequently rupture.

BROOK – School smart. Researches health stuff. Diagnosed with "small vagina." Has undiagnosed vestibulodynia.

CHARLIE – Almost popular. Diagnosed with PMS. Has undiagnosed ??? Charlie will never find out what's wrong.

AJ – New kid. Diagnosed with PMS/hormone issues. Has undiagnosed adrenal disorder.

HEALTHCARE PROFESSIONALS

ELLA – (she/her) – Receptionist. Bitter about all these teenagers. She's healthy gynecologically. But her birth control causes her migraines.

SERENA – Receptionist. Plays Ella's games, but secretly training to be a nurse. Has undiagnosed vestibulodynia.

DOCTOR – (she/her) – The doctor. Twenty-nine and overwhelmed. Has undiagnosed pregnancy. Also has undiagnosed need for a career change.

FAMILY MEMBERS

FAY – Charlie's older sibling. In college nearby. Gets dragged into babysitting Charlie. Has heavy periods that make Fay faint.

BABY – Mari's younger sibling. Mari sometimes has to babysit them while going to appointments. Any gender.

ENSEMBLE – As many other patients as you want in the waiting room. In the interludes, they become flash mobs and create silent scenes.

SETTING

A gynecologist's waiting room, half a block from the high school.

TIME

The present.

AUTHOR'S NOTES

Casting Notes

You'll notice that only Ella and Doc are listed as "she/her," and that in the script, the only pronouns referring to the rest of the cast are "theys" and "siblings" (which can be changed to reflect actor pronouns). You'll also notice that this play takes place in a gynecologist's waiting room, and most of the health conditions characters have are related to gynecologic organs. This eliminates ONLY cis men from most casting. Baby can be played by someone of any gender, including cis male, and cis men can be cast in the Ensemble as long as they are respectful of the subject matter.

For the roles of Mari, Brook, Zaz, Charlie, AJ, Fay, and Serena, anyone who has lived experience in a gynecologist's waiting room or hopes to in the future, they/she/he, is welcome.

Ella and the Doctor are cis women and may be played by anyone who feels comfortable playing a cis woman.

This play can be performed in any community, by people of any racial background. And, the problems of the gynecological medical system are compounded by racism and further disproportionately affect people of color. Consider casting the Doctor as a white actor and Mari and Fay (and as many of the cast as possible, ideally more than 50%) as Black or Latine.

If Mari and Fay are actors of color, use version A of Scene Three (imbedded in the script) to directly acknowledge the racism of the medical system. If Mari and Fay are white actors, use version B of Scene Three (included as an appendix).

A Note on The Flash Mob Interludes

Interludes A, B, and C can be sung, rapped, shown on posters, or spoken. The lines should be split between actors as you wish, and can be repeated at your discretion. Ideally, the interludes are energetic and stylized in some way. Depending on your ensemble's specific skills, for example, one could be a tap dance, one a cheer, one a power ballad, etc.

Allowable Changes to the Text

Feel free to change "TikTok" and "Reddit" to updated social media app names. You can also change "sucks" to "stinks" as needed.

Content Notes

This play is "clean" in that it doesn't contain swears, violence, or nudity onstage. The only physical touch called for in the script is a friendly hand-hold between Brook and Mari.

This play frankly discusses gynecological conditions, pelvic pain, and vaginas. Please share the script before auditions; chances are, half or more of your actors have some of the conditions dealt with in this script (and might not have heard about them before). This script is meant to help them feel seen and understood.

I ask you to place your teens' need for recognition and understanding over your adult audience members' need for comfort. Adult audiences might be shocked by this content, because our society doesn't allow for these crucial and ubiquitous health issues to be discussed in "polite conversation." But the lack of polite conversation about these health issues has prevented so many teens (and adults) from healing.

The question of this play is: how do we create community that helps us heal?

To Kalliope and Avery;

to teen Laura and teen Diane.

I love you.

Scene One

(The waiting room. **BROOK** *and* **ZAZ** *sit at opposite ends. It is completely silent.* **ZAZ** *has headphones in.)*

*(***BROOK*** *plugs in headphones and plays a video on a phone. Except* **BROOK** *doesn't push the headphone in far enough.)*

VIDEO. Do YOU have PAIN with SEX? Tune in to Doctor –

*(***BROOK*** *quickly turns it off.* **ZAZ** *is looking.)*

BROOK. I don't have pain with sex. I mean, I don't have sex. Please don't tell my mom I have sex. Please don't tell the soccer team I have sex. Please please don't tell the soccer team I have sex because you're on JV, right, so my mom is your coach and I really don't want my mom to think I have sex and if you tell the JV soccer team then it'll get back to my mom and I don't have pain with sex, okay, I just tried to put a tampon in and it really hurt so I was trying to do some research about why tampons hurt but I guess they just hurt, I don't know, I just tried tampons for the first time since I got my period because it hurt then and it hurts now and I guess I'm just doomed to wear pads for the rest of my life but I hate that and like eventually I guess I would like to have sex but not if it hurts but also again to be super clear I'm not having sex like I'd want to be in love or whatever or not in love but just have like a super clear communicative relationship with whoever I decide to have sex with but again I'm not even thinking about that like I'd really just like to be able to use a tampon slash not have part of my body be in excruciating pain.

*(**ZAZ** takes out a headphone.)*

ZAZ. What?

BROOK. Oh, wow, you didn't hear any of that?

ZAZ. Were you talking to me?

BROOK. Nope. Just doing my Duolingo.

ZAZ. Wait, do we have a test on Monday?

BROOK. What?

ZAZ. In Spanish. Why are you doing Duolingo?

BROOK. Oh, no reason, I just...like languages.

ZAZ. I mean, so do I, but like, do we have a test? 'Cause podemos practicar or whatever.

BROOK. NO. I mean, there's no test. Just that essay for next week.

ZAZ. Okay... They didn't call me, did they?

BROOK. Uh. No, I don't think so.

ZAZ. *(Totally lying.)* These headphones work, you know? I don't hear anything.

BROOK. I haven't seen anybody.

ZAZ. My appointment was like an hour ago.

BROOK. Mine too.

*(**ZAZ** puts headphones back in.)*

I'm gonna see if I can pee.

*(**BROOK** goes to the window.)*

Hi, excuse me? Um. Is there a bathroom I can use?

*(**ELLA** slides open the window.)*

ELLA. The doctor will see you shortly.

BROOK. Okay. Is there a –

ELLA. We're short-staffed today. I'll call you when she's ready.

BROOK. Thank you, I just wondered –

    (**ELLA** *slides the window shut again.*)

ZAZ. *(To* **BROOK**.*)* Bathroom's through that door. To the left, then the right.

BROOK. Thanks.

    (*Does* **BROOK** *clock that* **ZAZ** *was wearing headphones and heard that?*)

    (**BROOK** *exits toward the bathroom.*)

    (**FAY** *and* **CHARLIE** *come in.* **CHARLIE** *goes to sit near* **ZAZ**. **FAY** *goes to check* **CHARLIE** *in.*)

CHARLIE. Sup?

ZAZ. Dang, it got you too?

CHARLIE. The curse of going to the gynecologist?

ZAZ. I'm waiting on results. You think you have it?

CHARLIE. Have –

ZAZ. Herpes. Half the school has it, apparently. Stupid Shaun.

CHARLIE. Nooooo.

ZAZ. They're taking my blood.

CHARLIE. Bet they're gonna drink it.

    (*On the other side of the room:*)

FAY. Charlie with an I E.

SERENA. Uh-huh.

FAY. So Charlie's checked in?

SERENA. Aren't you the one with the fainting?

FAY. Yeah –

SERENA. You need to drink more iron.

FAY. Um, sure.

SERENA. Did you get those supplement drinks? Didn't I tell you last time, when you –?

FAY. Uh, yeah, they were backordered.

SERENA. Huh. Really?

FAY. Yeah. Do you know when the doctor will –

SERENA. Between you and me, it's gonna be a minute.

ELLA. And we go on lunch at 1:30.

FAY. I think it's already –

ELLA. LUNCH!

>   (**ELLA** *shuts the window.*)

>   (*On* **ELLA** *and* **SERENA**'s *side of the window:*)

One pregnant, one anxiety, two STDs, one PMS.

SERENA. That your final answer?

ELLA. I take my cupcake bets seriously.

SERENA. Pick your horses.

ELLA. The one in the bathroom is pregnant.

SERENA. The one in the bathroom?

ELLA. I said what I said.

SERENA. The one with the headphones is anxiety.

ELLA. And little sib's STD. First kid's results are clear, but little sib's results aren't.

SERENA. Bet kid coming in a minute is STD too.

ELLA. Kid coming in half an hour is PMS. Really, they all are.

SERENA. Except –

ELLA. Except the one in the bathroom. Pregnant.

> (**BROOK** *comes back from the bathroom and hesitates.*)

SERENA. THAT one?

ELLA. I'm telling you.

> (**BROOK** *comes to tentatively knock on the window.*)

> (**ELLA** *writes furiously on a piece of paper, sticks it on the outside of the window, and slams the window shut again.*)

BROOK. *(Reads.)* LUNCH TIL TWO P.M.

DO NOT KNOCK.

> (**BROOK** *goes back to a seat far from everyone.*)

ELLA. I work nine-hour days, I get half an hour and they think it's theirs too? They think they're special.

SERENA. So did we, once.

ELLA. Nah. I was never special. STD, anxiety, pregnant. In that order. As it should be.

SERENA. Why's that?

ELLA. The STD gives you anxiety and the kid teaches you you didn't know what anxiety was till they reached driving age.

SERENA. Ha.

*(In the waiting room, **BROOK** puts headphones in. Double-checks the headphones this time. Somehow still gets it wrong. From their phone, we hear:)*

VIDEO. Thanks for tuning in to learn about vestibulodynia. A common condition –

*(**BROOK** smashes the headphone into place, but...)*

[INTERLUDE A – VESTIBULODYNIA]

*(The **ENSEMBLE** suddenly jumps up from their waiting room chairs or rushes onstage to become a flash mob. All the named **CHARACTERS** can also jump up or enter from the wings and join the flash mob. They dance, they sing or chant, it's a whole phenomenon.)*

ENSEMBLE.
VEST-I-BUL-O-DYN-I-A
PAIN OF THE VAG-IIII-NA
TRY TO PUT SOMETHING IN-A-YA
YOU'LL START STRAIGHT-UP CRYYYY-ING
BUNCH OF WAYS THAT THIS COULD SHOW
COULD BE THERE FROM DAY ONE, BIRTH
REALLY, SORRY, NO ONE KNOWS
TRAUMA COULD HAVE MADE IT WORSE
COULD BE YOUR BACTERIA
LACT-O-BACT-I-LLI. SIGH.
TENSION MAKES YOU TEARY-UH
FIBROIDS OR G-I. I!
WE JUST KNOW IT HURTS!
                    HURTS!
HURTS!
        HURTS!
                HURTS!
                    HURTS!

IT'S OKAY, APPARENTLY
ONE IN EV'RY FOUR OR FIVE
OF VAGINAS SUFFER. WEIRD.
GOTTA BE A FIX TO TRY –

> *(The flash mob stops suddenly. If* **ELLA** *and* **SERENA** *joined in, they go back to their side of the window and slam it shut. If the* **DOCTOR** *joined in, she brings* **AJ** *to the back and slams that door shut. We are now in:)*

Scene Two

(**MARI, CHARLIE, ZAZ, FAY, BROOK,** *and* **BABY** *onstage. This is a different day.*)

BROOK. Getting dilators to stretch out the vagina??

(**MARI** *looks over.*)

MARI. What?

BROOK. Duolingo.

MARI. That's some weird Duolingo.

ZAZ. Chill. If Brook says it's Duolingo, then it is.

CHARLIE. Duolingo. I'm dead.

(**BABY** *looks up from across the room.*)

BABY. You're not dead.

CHARLIE. No, hun, I'm fine.

BABY. Charlie isn't dead.

CHARLIE. Correct.

ZAZ. I can't believe you have to bring Baby here.

MARI. Yah, like, I spend so much time at the gynecologist now, I have to bring my sibling??

CHARLIE. Sucks. SUCKS ALWAYS HAVING YOUR SIBLING AROUND.

(**FAY** *rolls eyes again.*)

FAY. Sucks having to babysit all the time.

MARI. Ohhhhhh –

CHARLIE. It's not like I NEED you here. Not like they're gonna say anything anyway. No one ever knows what's wrong with me.

(**AJ** *enters from the office. Goes to the window.*)

AJ. Hi. Checking out for AJ.

ZAZ. Who's that?

CHARLIE. New kid, I guess.

MARI. Hmm. They were in there a long time.

CHARLIE. Don't be judgey.

MARI. I wasn't being judgey!

CHARLIE. Uh-huh.

ZAZ. How did Shaun get to them already, if they're new?

CHARLIE. Not everyone has herpes. Not everyone makes out with stupid boys. Actually, I don't think really anyone has made out with Shaun.

(**ZAZ** *holds up their hands.*)

ZAZ. It was a dare.

MARI. I dunno, all the doc ever seems to do is give STD panels.

BROOK. That's a failure of the medical system, not an indication that we actually have STDs.

CHARLIE. Okay, Duolingo.

(**BROOK** *turns scarlet and goes back to pretending to not hear them.*)

MARI. You think it's finally my turn? What if I was actually dying?

FAY. Not sure it would make a difference.

(**AJ** *comes and sits down, ignoring everyone.*)

CHARLIE. (*Yelling towards the window.*) Hey, is it my turn? Charlie?

MARI. Definitely my turn. Mari. M A R I.

ZAZ. ZAZ HAS BEEN HERE THE LONGEST!

FAY. IF YOU COULD TAKE CHARLIE SOON THAT WOULD BE AWESOME so I can get out of here.

BABY. BABY'S TURN! IT'S BABY'S TURN!

MARI. YEAH, IT'S BABY'S OLDER SIBLING'S TURN! TAKE PITY ON THE CHILD!

BROOK. Stop it! You'll make them mad and it'll get slower. Just wait.

MARI. I've BEEN waiting.

ZAZ. I got here before you.

CHARLIE. Do you really wanna hurry up and get in there?

BROOK. *(To CHARLIE.)* You were just screaming with the rest of them.

ZAZ. *(To CHARLIE.)* No, but it's the principle of the thing. I was here first.

CHARLIE. I actually hate it when they take me in and they're not ready. Like they tell you to take off all your clothes and put on some paper trash thing and then you just wait.

MARI. Is there a rule, like, if they don't bring you in in an hour, you can leave?

ZAZ. It's not first period. You don't get points for showing up if the teacher ditches.

CHARLIE. Like you know when you're almost asleep, and your hand falls over the edge of the bed, and you don't wanna move it because that would bring you back to being awake, but you have to move it, because if you don't, the monster under the bed is gonna rise up and bite your hand off?

It's a real thing, don't act like you don't do it. Like humans are literally programmed not to dangle limbs over the sides of things because that's how you die.

It feels like that. When they tell you to get undressed and then you're just sitting in this freezing office with all these pointy-looking metal things and chairs they definitely don't sanitize and maybe a poster telling you to talk about sex with your doctor, like they tell you to dangle your vagina out there and then just leave you in the room with the monster.

I'd rather stay in the waiting room.

ZAZ. I mean, if you have like cervical cancer, it'll kill you either way.

MARI. Wow, Zaz.

ZAZ. Does Charlie LOOK like they got an HPV vaccine?? I'm just saying, you gotta go to the doctor eventually, you can't just like live in the waiting room.

MARI. We all got the HPV vaccine.

CHARLIE. I didn't.

MARI. For real?

ZAZ. Yeah, 'cause your mom's an anti-vaxxer.

CHARLIE. Shut up.

FAY. She is.

MARI. Ohhhhhh –

FAY. Doesn't mean you get to talk about my mom.

> (*Everyone goes quiet.*)

> (**FAY** *turns a page in a waiting-room magazine.*)

ZAZ. Yo. Your sibling's scary.

(**AJ** *puts in headphones.*)

(*Music up.**)

(*The waiting speeds up. The* **ENSEMBLE** *comes in and out, as our* **CAST MEMBERS** *cross and uncross their arms and legs, check the time, sigh loudly, etc. So much waiting. Finally most of them either get called in or leave in exasperation and we are left with…*)

---

* A license to produce *The Doctor Will See You Shortly* does not include a performance license for any third-party or copyrighted music. Licensees should create an original composition or use music in the public domain. For further information, please see the Music and Third-Party Materials Use Note on page iii.

Scene Three

(**FAY** *is in the waiting room alone.* **MARI** *comes out, looking stunned.*)

(**MARI** *kicks a chair. Then another.*)

FAY. Are you done?

(**MARI** *kicks another.*)

ELLA. *(From the office.)* Stop kicking my chairs or I'll kick you out!

(**MARI** *kicks one more but then subsides. Puts head in hands.*)

FAY. Um. Do you need me to call someone?

MARI. There's nothing wrong with me.

FAY. Whatever.

MARI. Constant periods, constant pain, weird discharge, did I mention the PAIN, and THERE'S NOTHING WRONG WITH ME. I don't even have herpes.

FAY. I can call your mom, maybe?

MARI. Why do I come here if all they do is gaslight me?

FAY. I wish I knew. They keep telling me to drink more iron.

MARI. I want to burn this place down. Or punch it down.

FAY. Maybe wait until Charlie's out.

MARI. Not actually. I'm not actually gonna –

FAY. I know.

MARI. How can my ultrasound be clear? With all of this – HOW CAN IT BE CLEAR? They told me I have anxiety. Maybe PMDD because of my anxiety.

Which the doctor said is "just severe PMS." It's just me tangling my stomach up in knots. It's just in my head. It's just, it's just, it's just, IT IS NOT JUST. I have anxiety. I've had anxiety forever, thank you childhood trauma, I'm already on an SSRI which is apparently the only treatment for PMDD anyway. THIS IS NOT THAT. THIS IS NOT ONLY THAT.

ELLA. *(From office.)* Hey, quiet down out there!

SERENA. *(From office to* **ELLA.***)* Ella, come on.

MARI. I need to know that I'm not secretly dying. And all I get is "your scans are clear, chill out."

FAY. That's what so many people get. Especially if you look like us. Gotta love a deeply racist medical system.

MARI. I know. But how else am I supposed to get a diagnosis?

FAY. Have you tried googling it?

MARI. Are you serious right now?

FAY. Look, it sucks, doctors are awful and the system's broken. I'm just saying, I found my diagnosis on Reddit.

MARI. Reddit??

FAY. Okay, kid, try TikTok or whatever.

MARI. I tried googling and all I got was "if you have severe abdominal pain go to the emergency room immediately."

FAY. You can't stop on the first page. I get it. You want someone in a white coat to help you through it and explain exactly what's happening, or at least you want the Internet to make it easy on the first try. I wanted that too. We deserve better. But this racist, sexist, transphobic system doesn't care what we deserve. So you have to keep looking. The only good part about millions of us dealing with this is that some of the millions are on Reddit and TikTok. Here, watch this.

*(**FAY** finds a video on their phone and hands it to **MARI**.)*

(Flash mob time.)

[INTERLUDE B – ENDO]

*(The **FLASH MOB** is back. Energetically. Because this one super sucks. Well, they all do.)*

*(Every actor and your **ENSEMBLE**, if you have one, bound onstage like this is a cheer competition.)*

ENSEMBLE.
EN-DO ME-TRI OHHH-SIS
CAN FEEL LIKE PSYCHOHHH-SIS
'CAUSE THE DOC SAYS OHHHH, SIS
SCANS ARE CLEAR, NO PAIN (WHAT??)
BUT YOU GOT THE PAIN (OH)
BLOOD COMES DOWN LIKE RAIN (OH)
RANDOM WEIGHT GAIN (YUP)
OR YOUR POOP FEELS STRAINED (OH)
IF YOUR PAIN IS STABBING STABBING
SO YOU FEEL LIKE STABBING STABBING
ONE OR MORE OF THE ABOVE,
COULD BE THIS THAT'S HAPP'NING, HAPP'NING
EN-DO ME-TRI OHHH-SIS
IT'S NOT CANCER, NOT JUST CYSTS
TISSUE OUTSIDE YOUR UTERUS
BRINGING ALL THE PAIN

*(The **FLASH MOB** dissipates, and we are left with the **DOCTOR** and **SERENA**.)*

Scene Four

*(The **DOCTOR** in the waiting room, head in her hands.)*

SERENA. Doc? Are you okay?

DOCTOR. Serena.

SERENA. I finished the patient notes. I was just turning off all the lights.

DOCTOR. Sure.

SERENA. Do you want me to...leave the lights on?

DOCTOR. No.

> *(**SERENA** waits for **DOCTOR** to leave. She doesn't.)*

SERENA. Long day?

DOCTOR. They all are.

SERENA. *(A throwaway agreement.)* Tell me about it. Have a good night, Doc –

> *(**SERENA** starts to leave. But **DOCTOR** says:)*

DOCTOR. I wish I could be back in the waiting room. It's stupid, no one wants to be a teenager again, but I do. Because when I was a teenager I still thought going to med school and becoming a doctor was going to fix something. I thought I was actually going to help people. And now I'm here, and I did all the right things, and I did this whole residency full of babies even though I don't care at all about obstetrics, and now I'm actually a gynecologist, and I just diagnose pregnancy and anxiety and STDs?

SERENA. Um. Those are important, but you're right, they're not –

DOCTOR. You could diagnose those. You do. I hear you and Ella.

SERENA. Oh, she's just joking around. I'm not –

DOCTOR. I wasn't trying to say it doesn't take skill. You can do it because you've been here so long.

SERENA. Two years.

DOCTOR. Longer than me. Longer than I'll stay.

SERENA. What did you think this job was?

DOCTOR. I thought I was going to see all of these exciting cancers and protrusions and deadly poison marbles that someone swallowed when they were five and are now stuck in a corner of their uterus, like that one episode of that hospital show. And instead it's just pregnancy, and anxiety, and STDs. And they all keep coming back. Teenager after teenager. I want to be a teenager so I can have common, easy to diagnose problems.

SERENA. What's your problem?

DOCTOR. I don't know. I have this strange set of symptoms I can't identify. We didn't cover this part in med school. It was all pregnancy and the associated hemorrhages. Or STDs and the associated dangers.

SERENA. And anxiety?

DOCTOR. No, that's just the diagnosis if nothing else looks wrong.

SERENA. That sounds...

>   (**DOCTOR** *throws up in a potted plant.*)

DOCTOR. I think I have a rare and complex uterine cancer.

>   (*The* **ENSEMBLE** *marches on.*)

>   (*They create a mass expanding out from the* **DOCTOR**.)

(As each member comes on, they start repeating the **DOCTOR**'s *words, until it builds to a gigantic overlapping cacophony.)*

ENSEMBLE. I think I have a rare and complex uterine cancer.

I think I have a rare and complex uterine cancer.

I think I have a rare and complex uterine cancer.

(The **ENSEMBLE** *mills and seethes around the stage until everyone exits but* **AJ** *and* **ELLA**.*)*

Scene Five

(**AJ** *storms into* **ELLA**'s *area.*)

AJ. You gave me the wrong results.

ELLA. Whoa. You can't be back here.

AJ. I need my results. For AJ.

ELLA. Step to your side of the window and we can talk.

AJ. THESE ARE NOT MY RESULTS.

ELLA. You want me to call security?

AJ. I want you to stop pretending this place has security and figure this out. I'm sorry I raised my voice. It's just, I'm not pregnant.

(**ELLA** *relaxes. And laughs.*)

ELLA. Honey, I've been where you are.

AJ. No, you really haven't.

ELLA. Okay, I shouldn't have laughed. But I didn't realize THOSE were the results you thought were mixed up. It happens all the time. It happened to me. You're using a (*Lowers her voice.*) balloon – but it broke, or you took your magic pill a little late and –

AJ. I don't have vaginal intercourse.

ELLA. Wow. You talk to your mother with that mouth?

AJ. I'm using medical terminology about my own body...

ELLA. Your generation. Results don't lie. You're pregnant.

AJ. Please check.

ELLA. You want the blood test again.

AJ. Please check. If there's any way my results got mixed up with the next person who got blood drawn. Because I swear to you, it is physically impossible that I am pregnant.

(**ELLA** *sighs.*)

ELLA. All right, I guess you're PROCESSING or whatever…

(*She rolls her chair over to some files.*)

You were the only one who got blood drawn after three p.m. that day. So.

(*The* **DOCTOR** *comes in.*)

DOCTOR. Ella, I need a break, I'm so nauseous. I keep throwing up and I don't know why. Especially in the mornings.

(**ELLA** *and* **AJ** *exchange glances.*)

ELLA. Doc, you didn't do a blood draw couple nights ago, did you?

DOCTOR. I probably have a rare and complex uterine cancer. Of course I did a blood draw.

ELLA. You don't ever get the labels right on your own…

(**ELLA** *takes the results from* **AJ**'s *hands and gives them to the* **DOCTOR**.)

AJ. Did the results show anything?

DOCTOR. Wow, thank you for caring! Clinically high cortisol. But that's just stress from being in the medical industry, I guess.

AJ. You're a DOCTOR, don't you know that isn't how that works?

ELLA. Look at your results, Doc.

DOCTOR. I just told you –

ELLA. I didn't hand you that file for fun.

(*The* **DOCTOR** *looks at the file* **ELLA** *handed her.*)

DOCTOR. I'm pregnant?

(Music up.)*

(The **DOCTOR** *takes off her white coat and goes and sits in the waiting room, waiting for her own appointment in a different doctor's office.)*

(The **ENSEMBLE** *joins her, in and out, as they cross and uncross their arms and legs, check the time, sigh loudly, etc. So much waiting. The* **DOCTOR** *exits midway through to her appointment, as the* **ENSEMBLE** *continues to wait, in and out, arms crossing and uncrossing. We are back in this waiting room. Finally...)*

Scene Six

(**BROOK**, **MARI**, *and* **BABY**. *Waiting.*)

(*Total silence. Until* **BABY** *gets bored and goes up to* **BROOK**.)

BABY. Hi, what's wrong with you?

BROOK. Um. Hi...

(*Looks to* **MARI**, *but* **MARI** *ignores everything.*)

I don't know what's wrong with me. And it isn't nice to just ask people personal questions like that.

BABY. Why not?

BROOK. Um. It could be something I don't want to talk about.

BABY. Okay. Why don't you talk to my sibling?

BROOK. Two for two.

BABY. Mari's nice. Just pretends to not be.

BROOK. I'm sure Mari is nice, we're just not friends. Not everyone likes everyone. Especially when you're the weird kid who's constantly missing school for pain.

BABY. But you could like each other. If you tried.

BROOK. Okay, sure.

BABY. So go try.

BROOK. You're serious.

BABY. Mari's having a bad day. It would be great if you could be nice to Mari. And it's not like you were doing anything else.

BROOK. Just researching on Reddit to try to figure out, you know, if I'm going to live to go to college...

BABY. Pleeeease.

> (**BROOK** *goes over to* **MARI**'s *side of the room.*)

BROOK. Hi.

> (**MARI** *keeps looking down at their phone.*)

Your sibling wants me to say hi to you. They think you're having a bad day.

MARI. Thanks, I guess.

BROOK. Do you want to talk about it?

MARI. No offense, but I only know you from math class, so like...

BABY. So get to know each other. It's not that hard. Favorite color, favorite movie. That's what my teacher has us do.

> (**BABY** *goes back to "ignoring" them.*)

MARI. How do I look so awful that my kid sibling is trying to make me a friend?

BROOK. Not doing great over here either. I think this place does that.

MARI. Yeah. What are you in for?

BROOK. No idea. They tested me for –

MARI. Pregnancy, anxiety, and STDs?

BROOK. Yeah.

MARI. Same.

BROOK. What do you think you actually have?

MARI. Can we do favorite colors instead?

BROOK. Oh. Sure.

MARI. It's just, I'm sitting over here obsessing and it feels like you kind of are too, so maybe let's just do what Baby said?

BROOK. Blue. Cyan blue. Like the really bright deep one.

MARI. Pink.

BROOK. PINK?!?

MARI. No, obviously black.

> *(They laugh.)*

Pink is actually cute, but I can't find anything that goes with the outfit.

BROOK. You ever think about neon highlights?

MARI. What is this, the nineties?

BROOK. Okay, never mind, obviously I'm not the fashionista.

MARI. Obviously you're not, you say "fashionista."

BROOK. Right.

> **(BROOK** *looks uncomfortable and starts to move away.)*

MARI. I didn't mean – look, sarcasm is like my go-to. I don't really read people? But then sometimes I guess I make other people feel bad? But then, I don't know, it seems like everyone else says the same things I say, but like it's fun when they do it and wrong when I do? But also I'm about to get my period, well in two weeks, and two weeks before my period it also starts to feel like the world is literally collapsing on itself and nothing is ever going to be okay again? And two weeks before my period is like half my life 'cause I get my period every four weeks? And if half my life is collapsing on itself and catastrophizing then isn't that basically my life? Also I literally can't trust doctors to care about my period or my pain or even my life? Also I think I'm having a panic attack?

BROOK. Can I hold your hands?

MARI. Yeah.

> (**BROOK** *takes* **MARI***'s hands. They breathe together.*)

BROOK. Look, I can't tell you it's gonna be okay –

MARI. Thanks.

BROOK. I don't know what's going on with your body, I don't know what's going on with mine. But I can hold your hands and breathe with you. You're here, you're safe right now, you're currently okay.

MARI. *(Doing the 5 4 3 2 1 grounding exercise.)* Bent edge of that chair. Potted plant. Baby. Old magazines. You.

BROOK. Brook.

MARI. Brook. That's five. Four. Your hand. The draft from the AC. Dry mouth. Chain digging into my thigh. Three. The lights humming. Me breathing. Brook breathing. Two. This gross carpet. Baby's goldfish. One. Um.

> (**BABY** *grabs the goldfish and hands them to* **MARI**. **MARI** *chews one.*)

Your snack. Thank you, Baby. Thank you, Brook. Sorry.

BROOK. You don't need to apologize.

MARI. You think I'm a total nutcase.

BROOK. I think you're living with anxiety and managing it like a pro.

MARI. You talk like a teacher.

BROOK. Better than talking like a goth teenager.

> *(They laugh. After a pause:)*

The doctor told me I have a small vagina. And that's why everything hurts so much.

MARI. Seriously?

> *(They laugh harder.)*

My favorite movie is the old one, with the old guy, with the balloons? And the dog under the porch.

BROOK. I like the one about all the emotions coming to life.

> (**BROOK** *does something really dorky, like the Star Trek salute.*)

Fellow old movie lover, I greet you.

MARI. Oh babe, no.

> (**MARI** *teaches* **BROOK** *how to do something else celebratory/introductory here, like a salute or hand gesture. Let your* **ENSEMBLE** *define what this is for them.*)

> *(This transition is for connections between* **ENSEMBLE MEMBERS***. The creation of a secret handshake between fellow sufferers. Maybe this grows into a combo of several different TikTok dances. But in the end, it's still waiting. Until we land with:)*

Scene Seven

(**ZAZ** *and* **CHARLIE** *and* **AJ**.)

ZAZ. Honestly, they're just padding the bill at this point.

CHARLIE. Two different visits for blood and a urine sample.

ZAZ. Like, joke's on you, my mom's insurance will haggle you down to like a dollar a visit.

CHARLIE. How do you even know about this stuff?

ZAZ. Oh. I actually handle a lot of it for my family... My mom had to get a hysterectomy from her fibroids, so...

CHARLIE. Hidden depths, Zaz. Sorry.

ZAZ. Sure.

AJ. Your results might not even be right.

CHARLIE. What?

AJ. They told me I was pregnant.

ZAZ. Wow, new kid, way to come in with a bang.

AJ. You're gross, and I didn't. Look, you seem like not my type of friends, but I'm gonna tell you on principle, they mixed up my results. With the doctor's. Like how incompetent can you even get? And. Turns out they give two different kinds of blood tests. There's the basic teenager panel, STDs, pregnancy, you know, and then there's the complex all-the-things panel, if they're actually looking for something, the one we don't get, where you can get hits for high cortisol, for adrenal disorders, and T and estrogen, for hormone imbalance, and thyroid stuff. The doctor was just giving us the basic pregnancy one. That's probably why you're back, because they're afraid I'm gonna sue them for the result swap.

ZAZ. Are you?

AJ. No. What junior in high school has that kind of money? Just, double check everything, is what I'm saying.

CHARLIE. That's...bad.

ZAZ. I mean, it's pretty obvious.

CHARLIE. Okay, Zaz know-everything-about-the-healthcare-system-suddenly.

ZAZ. Why would they test us for everything, when they can just diagnose us with PMS and send us home? Teenagers rarely die from physical pain. I should know, I have stabbing pain in my abdomen all the time, and like, eventually it goes away for a while.

CHARLIE. That's grim.

AJ. So, what, we just chill here, wait forever, get results that don't mean anything, and then go suffer?

ZAZ. Basically.

AJ. Nope.

CHARLIE. Yeah, no. Not excited about that.

AJ. *(To* **ZAZ**.*)* Look, I don't really like you, and I'm sure you actually have herpes, but your stabbing pain thing sounds real and unrelated. You really wanna let them tell you it's only herpes?

ZAZ. Are there other...options?

CHARLIE. Down to make one up.

[INTERLUDE C – OVARIAN CYSTS]

(The **FLASH MOB** *explodes onto the scene again. Maybe I shouldn't use the word explodes, because...)*

ENSEMBLE.
OHHHH
–VARIAN CYSTS ARE SACS OF FLUID
VERY COMMON, FOLLICLES DO IT
MOST CYSTS START OUT AS BENIGN
WHEN THEY GROW THERE ARE BIG SIGNS
TEN OF TEN ABDOMINAL PAIN
FEELING LIKE YOUR OVARY'S STRAINED
IF YOUR ULTRASOUND SHOWS CLEAR
NURSE WILL SHRUG, IT'S OVER, DEAR
RUPTURED, IT WENT ON ITS OWN
GO ON, PAY, AND LEAVE ALONE
THING ABOUT THE CYSTS THOUGH IS
CYSTS ON CYSTS ON CYSTS ON CYSTS
IF YOU GOT ONE CYST THAT BROKE
MORE ARE COMING, AREN'T YOU STOKED?
GOTTA HOPE THIS ONE WON'T GROW (TOO)
BIG BEFORE IT JUST EXPLODES.
POW!

> (The **ENSEMBLE** *explodes off the scene. Yeah,*
> *they're tasteless.*)

Scene Eight

> (*The sit-in.* **AJ, CHARLIE, ZAZ, MARI, BROOK, FAY, BABY,** *and the whole* **ENSEMBLE** *are having a "symptom party" in the waiting room. Does someone decorate? Maybe they lay out blankets and pillows on the floor. They take over the space.*)

> (**ELLA** *and* **SERENA** *on the other side of the desk.*)

ELLA. Are they even on the schedule?

SERENA. A couple of them called, but I told them we were booked.

ELLA. Then what are they doing here?

SERENA. I think maybe they're doing something.

> (*In the main room,* **FAY** *picks up a bullhorn – a bullhorn!! – and speaks through it.*)

FAY. ANYBODY IN WALKING DISTANCE. IF YOU HAVE GYNECOLOGICAL SYMPTOMS YOU DON'T UNDERSTAND, COME ON DOWN TO OUR SYMPTOM PARTY. WE'RE GONNA SHARE WHAT'S GOING ON WITH US AND TALK THIS OUT WITH THE FINE ASSISTANCE OF TIKTOK AND REDDIT AND ALSO JSTOR BECAUSE I'M IN COLLEGE NOW, LOSERS.

ELLA. No way. Come on.

SERENA. Comparing symptoms and researching diagnoses? Sounds useful, actually.

ELLA. Are you serious? We need to get them out of here.

SERENA. Really, Ella?

ELLA. Security isn't in my job description, but I guess it is now. And it's almost one-thirty.

> (**ELLA** *and* **SERENA** *come into the main room.*
> **DOCTOR** *comes out from the back.*)

DOCTOR. Are we this overbooked? Is there any way we can reschedule some –

> (**BROOK** *grabs the bullhorn.*)

BROOK. YOU'RE NOT OVERBOOKED. YOU'RE UNDERDELIVERING. SO WE'RE HERE TO TALK TO EACH OTHER AND THE INTERNET AND FIGURE OUT WHAT WE HAVE.

ELLA. Sit DOWN, child. You have PMS like everyone else. You're not special.

CHARLIE. You really think every person with a vagina deserves to suffer random debilitating symptoms for half their lives? Because I don't think I "just have PMS."

ELLA. I think life hurts and you already got your blood tests, so –

SERENA. SHUT UP.

ZAZ. Plot twist.

SERENA. Shut up, Ella. Not everyone just has PMS. I know you have seniority in the office and I've tried to do things the way you want to do them, but the way you want to do them sucks. It's not always STD, anxiety, pregnancy, in that order. Okay, maybe some of the time. But most of the time, it's because we're shoehorning these kids' symptoms into easy boxes so we can medicate them and send them home because after all, they're teenagers, they're people with vaginas, they must just be complaining. You know what? That sucks. You suck. This place sucks. If I didn't need the money for my night classes I would've quit a long time ago. People deserve care. That's why I'm becoming a nurse.

It's why you should be working here, that and benefits because capitalism. People deserve care. And these kids are people, and so am I, and I for one am sick of getting sent home from an excruciating pap smear being told "I must not have enough sex" or "getting pregnant should fix that." I'm sick of underestimating everyone, including myself. And I know you "never get sick" and have a stunningly perfect uterus but your migraines could be from your birth control. So sit down, shut up, and LISTEN.

     (**SERENA** *sits down in the circle.*)

     (**ELLA** *follows.*)

     (*So does the* **DOCTOR**.)

     (**MARI** *takes the bullhorn.*)

MARI. THANK YOU – (what's your name?)

SERENA. Serena.

MARI. THANK YOU SERENA. WE APPRECIATE YOU. I JUST WANTED TO USE THE BULLHORN.

     (**MARI** *puts the bullhorn down.*)

BROOK. All right. Who wants to start?

End of Play

APPENDIX

Scene Three: Version B

(Use this version of the scene if **FAY** *and* **MARI** *are played by white actors.)*

*(**FAY** is in the waiting room alone. **MARI** comes out, looking stunned.)*

*(**MARI** kicks a chair. Then another.)*

FAY. Are you done?

> *(**MARI** kicks another.)*

ELLA. *(From the office.)* Stop kicking my chairs or I'll kick you out!

> *(**MARI** kicks one more but then subsides. Puts head in hands.)*

FAY. Um. Do you need me to call someone?

MARI. There's nothing wrong with me.

FAY. Whatever.

MARI. Constant periods, constant pain, weird discharge, did I mention the PAIN, and THERE'S NOTHING WRONG WITH ME. I don't even have herpes.

FAY. I can call your mom, maybe?

MARI. Why do I come here if all they do is gaslight me?

FAY. I wish I knew. They keep telling me to drink more iron.

MARI. I want to burn this place down. Or punch it down.

FAY. Maybe wait until Charlie's out.

MARI. Not actually. I'm not actually gonna –

FAY. I know.

MARI. How can my ultrasound be clear? With all of this – HOW CAN IT BE CLEAR? They told me I have anxiety. Maybe PMDD because of my anxiety. Which the doctor said is "just severe PMS." It's just me tangling my stomach up in knots. It's just in my head. It's just, it's just, it's just, IT IS NOT JUST. I have anxiety. I've had anxiety forever, thank you childhood trauma, I'm already on an SSRI which is apparently the only treatment for PMDD anyway. THIS IS NOT THAT. THIS IS NOT ONLY THAT.

ELLA. *(From office.)* Hey, quiet down out there!

SERENA. *(From office to **ELLA**.)* Ella, come on.

MARI. I need to know that I'm not secretly dying. And all I get is "your scans are clear, chill out."

FAY. Have you tried googling it?

MARI. Are you serious right now?

FAY. Look, it sucks, doctors are awful and the system's broken. I'm just saying, I found my diagnosis on Reddit.

MARI. Reddit??

FAY. Okay, kid, try TikTok or whatever.

MARI. I tried googling and all I got was "if you have severe abdominal pain go to the emergency room immediately."

FAY. You can't stop on the first page. I get it. You want someone in a white coat to help you through it and explain exactly what's happening, or at least you want the Internet to make it easy on the first try. I wanted that too. We deserve better. But this system doesn't care what we deserve. So you have to keep looking. The only good part about millions of us dealing with this is that some of the millions are on Reddit and TikTok. Here, watch this.

*(**FAY** finds a video on their phone and hands it to **MARI**.)*

(Flash mob time.)

The Odds Are...

by Dennis A. Allen II

THE ODDS ARE... premiered with Keen Company (Jonathan Silverstein, Artistic Director) as part of the Keen Teens Festival of New Work at Theatre Row in New York City on May 17, 2024. The performance was directed by Antu Yacob, with sets by Yi-Hsuan (Ant) Ma and Yun Yen, costumes by Dan Wang, lights by Hayley Garcia Parnell, sound by Eden Segbefia, and props by Caitlyn Murphy. The Production Stage Manager was Sloane Fischer. The cast was as follows:

JASMINE	Lavelle Price
THEO	George Henry
BENJAMIN	Tai Duong
ANGELINA	Aishwarya (Ria) Joseph
ANGEL	Dasan Turner
ROXY	Viktoriia Yatsyshyna
MARIE	Nicole Lerman
MEWS	Charlotte Coffey
SERENITY	August Eaves
GIANNA	Stephanie Solis-Romero

CHARACTERS

JASMINE – athletic, Black American, Female, sixteen

THEO – extrovert, Black, Male, seventeen

BENJAMIN – type A personality, Male, nineteen

ANGELINA – assertive, Female, sixteen

ANGEL – whimsical, Male, sixteen

ROXY – perfectionist, Female, fifteen

MARIE – codependent, Female, fifteen

MEWS – coquettish, Nonbinary masculine presenting, seventeen

SERENITY – self righteous, Female, fifteen

GIANNA – angsty, Female, seventeen

SETTING

The GARY Center, Upstate NY.

TIME

Very Near Future.

AUTHOR'S NOTES

// indicates dialogue is cut off

This play moves at a quick pace. The transitions and dialogue should be fluid, so a minimalistic approach to staging and props best serves the play.

1. The Hand

(In the dark, nature sounds fill the space. The wind rustling leaves, a far-off waterfall gently rumbles, frogs and crickets and birds, oh my. As the lights dawn we find ourselves on the grounds of the Gambling Addiction Rehabilitation Youth Center, located in way out there somewhere ain't nobody ever been, New York. **ANGIE** *and* **ANGEL** *are sitting on the ground motionless, intensely staring up at the sky.)*

BENJAMIN. *(Offstage.)* Welcome to the Gambling Addiction Rehabilitation Youth Center or the GARY Center for short.

> *(***BENJAMIN*** *enters holding a clipboard.* ***JASMINE*** *and* ***THEO*** *follow close behind, each have a rolling suitcase.)*

Over here you'll find our main building.

Did you know that even though we've only been operating for three years the GARY Center is the most successful addiction recovery facility in the United States.

JASMINE. Says who? By what standard?

THEO. Wow, it's really quiet out here.

BENJAMIN. WE have the lowest recidivism rate in the country.

THEO. *(Facetiously.)* Fascinating.

THEO. Can we really not have our phones the entire thirty days?

JASMINE. Lowest recidivism?

BENJAMIN. Recidivism means //

JASMINE. I know what recidivism is, but I don't know if you do.

THEO. I know I don't.

JASMINE. A person's relapse into criminal behavior.

THEO. Um, I am not a criminal. Just impulsive.

Oo, are we gonna be with any celebrities?

BENJAMIN. I can assure you, of all the facilities popping up around the country, both private and public, ours is the most successful in rehabilitating youth gambling addicts.

JASMINE. Okay but //

BENJAMIN. This building here to the right is where our dining hall is //

JASMINE. This is a rehab center.

BENJAMIN. It is.

JASMINE. People choose to come here.

BENJAMIN. Indeed.

JASMINE. So you can't tout people not coming back.

BENJAMIN. *(Knowingly.)* Did you choose to come here?

> (**BENJAMIN** *flips up a page on his clipboard in a performative manner as if reading the answer to his question.)*

THEO. Oop! Shade.

Wait, are you being forced to be here?

I thought that was illegal?

BENJAMIN. Everything in life is a choice.

JASMINE. *(Pointedly.)* Free will's a fairytale for children.

THEO. Damn.

BENJAMIN. Did you know that the prefrontal cortex isn't fully mature until we turn thirty?

THEO. You are full of fun facts. About our phones //

JASMINE. How old are you?

BENJAMIN. Look, Jasmine. Theodore...

THEO. Theo.

BENJAMIN. I get it. I'm a former inmate myself.

I mean I'm not but I am.

Not an actual inmate. I've been through the program here.

This is not prison.

It's paradise.

THEO. O. KAY.

So where's the nearest bodega? I gots to stock up on my snacks.

(**BENJAMIN** *laughs.*)

BENJAMIN. The closest store is over twenty miles away. There's a shuttle that comes here every other day but only staff are allowed to board it. Every single minute of your thirty days here must be spent within the facility's perimeter.

THEO. Uh huh.

BENJAMIN. As I was saying before, the dining hall is there, it is well stocked and Did you know we have Michelin star chefs, the best in the country, preparing our meals? Also you'll find the exercise room, a sauna and steam room, a screening room for movie nights and our meditation rooms on the basement level.

JASMINE. I don't see any basketball courts or tennis courts they inside too?

THEO. Oo, pickle ball?!

BENJAMIN. No, we don't support the playing of sports of any kind here.

JASMINE. Seriously?

BENJAMIN. No cellphones. No computers. No internet. No TVs. We encourage you all to stay away from all things competitive. No cards no dice no boardgames of any kind.

THEO. *(To **JASMINE**.)* Not even Monopoly?

BENJAMIN. You must attend all of your individual therapy sessions and the group sessions and outings. We keep a very regimented schedule. When you go on hikes you are required to wear the facility's red shirts. Three shirts will be issued to you by the end of today, if you want more you have to purchase them.

THEO. *(Facetiously.)* Oh this is clearly not prison.

BENJAMIN. I strongly suggest you take a close look at the "Dos and Don'ts" section of your welcome packets. We adhere to a three strike system here.

JASMINE. *(To **BENJAMIN**.)* So baseball terminology but no baseball?

BENJAMIN. *(To **JASMINE**.)* *You especially* should take this seriously. Three violations and you're out.

JASMINE. Got it.

BENJAMIN. I'll be your cohort's facility leader.

JASMINE. *Mr.* Benjamin, how old are you?

BENJAMIN. Benjamin's fine.

Old enough.

THEO. What the hell is a cohort?

JASMINE. Like a group.

THEO. Okay so no cellphones or internet in the middle of nowhere with the closest civilization over twenty miles away?

It's giving every horror movie ever made.

BENJAMIN. The only thing that should feel fear are those gambling demons you've got inside you.

> (**BENJAMIN** *laughs awkwardly.*)

THEO. Okay now I'm legit scared.

> (**BENJAMIN** *sees* **ANGIE** *and* **ANGEL**.)

BENJAMIN. These two will be a part of your cohort.

What are you two doing?

> (**ANGIE** *and* **ANGEL** *pop up like they've been caught doing something they shouldn't.*)

ANGIE. *(To* **BENJAMIN**.*)* DieKayKay!

ANGEL. DieKayKay's here?

BENJAMIN. Please stop calling me that.

ANGIE. Kay Kay darling you've brought us new sacrifices.

ANGEL. Fresh meat.

ANGIE. I'm Angelina, you can call me Angie. This is Angel.

ANGEL. I'm Angel. You can call me Angel.

JASMINE. Jasmine.

THEO. Theo.

ANGIE. Jasmine you look familiar. I know you?

JASMINE. Nope.

BENJAMIN. What were you two just doing?

ANGEL. Sun bathing.

ANGIE. Getting that good ol' vitamin D.

(**ANGIE** *giggles childishly.*)

BENJAMIN. Fully clothed?

ANGEL. Sensitive skin.

ANGIE. It's like I need that vitamin D but I'm always getting burnt.

THEO. Story of my life.

BENJAMIN. Did you know that low levels of vitamin D is a major cause of depression?

THEO. Story of my life.

(*Four of them laugh.* **BENJAMIN** *doesn't get it.*)

BENJAMIN. Depression is nothing to laugh about.

Would you two finish showing them around please. I have to use the little boys' room.

ANGEL. That's gross.

BENJAMIN. It's a biological necessity.

ANGEL. Calling it "the little boys' room." You're too old for that bro.

BENJAMIN. It's a euphemism.

ANGEL. Eww.

BENJAMIN. Did you know in the Greek eu means "well" and phēmē means "speaking"?

ANGEL. What's the Greek for, don't nobodycareabout whatyoutalkinabout?

(**ANGEL** *and* **ANGIE** *laugh.* **BENJAMIN** *begrudgingly exits.*)

THEO. What is a DieKayKay?

ANGIE. You'll figure it out.

ANGEL. She'll get it first.

ANGIE. Oh you wanna bet?

ANGEL. Why yes. Yes I do.

ANGIE. I bet you a week of chores Theo here figures out the meaning of DieKayKay first.

ANGEL. Deal.

I won by the way.

ANGIE. What?

You did not!

ANGEL. You looked away from the sun first.

ANGIE. If I didn't Benjamin would've caught us.

ANGEL. So?! Pay up.

> (**ANGIE** *tosses* **ANGEL** *a bag of Sour Patch Kids.*[*])

JASMINE. I'm staying away from you two.

ANGEL. Judgy.

You ain't a snitch are you?

JASMINE. Hardly.

THEO. Excuse me, but did you say chores?

ANGIE. Along with the "nature immersion" and "tech deprivation," this center believes "responsibility reinforces rehabilitation."

THEO. Wow. I don't do chores. How do you even know we'll have chores?

---

[*] A license to produce *The Odds Are...* does not include a license to publicly display any branded logos or trademarked images. Licensees must acquire rights for any logos and/or images or create their own.

ANGIE. This is me and Angel's third time at this fine establishment.

    (*To* **JASMINE**.) They're pretty strict around here about anything that resembles gambling.

THEO. Third time?! Isn't that revid–? //

JASMINE. Exactly. Look. What you do is none of my business.

    Like I said, I'm staying away.

ANGEL. Why are YOU here Judgy?

        (**ANGEL** *starts sniffing* **JASMINE** *all over.*)

    I'm thinking Blackjack. No! Poker. Online Poker. No. Blackjack. Final answer.

JASMINE. No.

ANGEL. Oh then it must be you...

        (**ANGEL** *moves towards* **THEO**.)

THEO. Sniff at me and I will snatch your nose right off your face.

        (**ANGEL** *growls at* **THEO**. **THEO** *puts his fists up in a fighting stance.*)

ANGIE. Come here Angel. Heel heel. Sit.

        (**ANGEL** *sits by* **ANGIE** *like dog.* **ANGIE** *pets his head.*)

JASMINE. Y'all are weird.

ANGIE. You're my little weirdo. Yes you are. Yes you are.

        (**ANGEL** *gets on his back and* **ANGIE** *pats his stomach like you would a dog. They are indeed weird.*)

JASMINE. Is everyone here as messed up as you two.

ANGIE. You *are* Judgy. Come on Angel, lets take'm on a walkabout.

> *(With **ANGEL** still committed to the dog routine he and **ANGIE** exit.)*

THEO. Are we gonna die out here?

JASMINE. *I'm* not.

> *(**JASMINE** exits.)*

THEO. Why'd you say "I'm" like that?

You know something I don't know?

> *(**THEO** exits. Transition.)*

2. The Action

(**ROXY**, **MARIE**, **MEWS**, **SERENITY** *and* **GIANNA** *enter.* **SERENITY** *sits holding her Bible out and up towards* **MEWS** *who stands over* **SERENITY** *like he's chastising her.*)

(**GIANNA** *pretends to read a* Vogue *magazine as she observes* **MEWS** *and* **SERENITY**'s *interaction.*[*] **ROXY** *and* **MARIE** *rehearse a TikTok-style dance routine.*)

MEWS.	SERENITY.
Not saying I'm THE God, we're all Gods	The good book says different!

SERENITY. It's literally the First Commandment.

MEWS. The First Commandment is you shall have no OTHER gods before me.

SERENITY. Yeah!

MEWS. Right. So it says that other gods exist just you can't choose them over the one.

SERENITY. Leave me alone. Let me read in peace.

MEWS. I'm just trying to engage you in a healthy debate.

SERENITY. Who said I want to debate with you?

MEWS. People that walk around holding the Bible usually love to defend their faith.

SERENITY. I'm not people. I'm me. So please.

(*A moment.*)

---

[*] A license to produce *The Odds Are...* does not include a license to publicly display any branded logos or trademarked images. Licensees must acquire rights for any logos and/or images or create their own.

MEWS. Have you ever considered God doesn't exist?

(**SERENITY** *puts her fingers in her ears.*)

SERENITY. *(Sings.)*
ANGELS WE HAVE HEARD ON HIGH
SWEETLY SINGING O'ER THE PLAINS,

(**ROXY** *and* **MARIE** *stop rehearsing and look towards* **SERENITY**. **GIANNA** *pretends to ignore.*)

AND THE MOUNTAINS IN REPLY
ECHOING THEIR JOYOUS STRAINS.
GLOOOOOOOOOOOOOOOOOOOOOOORIA,
IN EXCELSIS DEO!

MEWS. I'm just saying...

SERENITY.
GLOOOOOOOOOOOOOOOOOOOOOOORIA,
IN EXCELSIS DEO!

MEWS. Okay I get it!

I'm sorry.

SERENITY. Thank you.

GIANNA. That was childish.

SERENITY. Well I'm a child.

Of God.

GIANNA. Cute.

MEWS. Roxy. Marie. What do you think?

ROXY.	**MARIE.**
We're busy	Dancing

(*They go back to their routine.*)

MEWS. Gianna, what do you believe?

(**GIANNA** *stares at* **MEWS** *over the magazine. A moment of silent stare.*)

MEWS. Gianna? Gia?!

GIANNA. I'm sorry like, I didn't know you knew I existed.

(**ROXY** *and* **MARIE** *giggle without missing a step in their routine.*)

MEWS. Come on Gia don't be like that.

GIANNA. Be like what? Like how you always have me left on read?

MEWS. Why are you bringing up old stuff in a new space? I swear I would reply to your DMs in my mind.

(**ROXY** *and* **MARIE** *laugh again. Still dancing.* **GIANNA** *raises her magazine to hide her anger and embarrassment.*)

SERENITY. You see Mews, nobody wants to hear your devilish tongue.

GIANNA. Oh like, shut up Serenity! Serenity. That's probably like not even your real name.

(**GIANNA** *storms out.*)

SERENITY. What did I do?

MEWS. Nothing. It's not you.

SERENITY. Oh. Well I'll pray that she finds peace.

ROXY. No Marie! Damnit!

MARIE. Don't yell at me!

ROXY. It's, here. Here. Uh. Uh. Uh. THEN spin, switch.

MARIE. It would be easier if we had music.

ROXY. But we don't. Do we?

MARIE. Don't get nasty.

ROXY. I'm sorry.

I can't believe we can't have our phones at all. So stupid. Stupid!

MARIE. It's okay. Let's do it again.

> (**ROXY** *and* **MARIE** *do the dance routine.* **JASMINE** *and* **THEO** *enter.*)

THEO. *(To* **ROXY** *and* **MARIE.***)* Ayyyyyye! Get it get it get it.

> (**THEO** *joins the dance attempting to learn* **MARIE** *and* **ROXY**'*s routine in real time. After a moment* **MEWS** *sees* **JASMINE** *and walks over to her.*)

MEWS. *(Sultry.)* Hi.

JASMINE. Sup.

MEWS. I'm Mews.

JASMINE. Muse like inspiration from the gods?

MEWS. Yeah, kind of. Spelled different.

JASMINE. Cool.

MEWS. What's your name?

JASMINE. *(To the room.)* Excuse me, have any of you seen Angie and Angel. They were supposed to be showing us around.

THEO. Yeah, these fools were showing us the hiking trails then just ran off without a word.

MEWS. I'd stay away from those two. They are, odd.

SERENITY. Aren't we all? Hi, I'm Serenity.

THEO. Theo.

MARIE. Marie.

ROXY. Roxy.

*(They look at **JASMINE**.)*

JASMINE. Can someone show me where we sleep please?

SERENITY. I can take you.

JASMINE. Thank you.

Theo I'll see you later.

THEO. Okay darling.

> *(**JASMINE** and **SERENITY** exit.)*

MEWS. Bye.

> *(**MEWS** goes immediately to **THEO**.)*

Are you two friends?

THEO. We just met on the *six hour bus ride* here from the city.

Total trauma bonding.

ROXY. Bus? Like a private party bus?

THEO. Girl I wish. My mother thought it would teach me to appreciate life or something. I am starving.

MARIE. Roxy and I can go with you to the café.

THEO. Amazing.

ROXY. See you later Mews.

THEO. Muse? Like divine inspiration?

MEWS. Yeah but spelled different.

THEO. *(Facetiously.)* Fascinating.

Let's go my dancing divas.

> *(**THEO**, **MARIE** and **ROXY** exit. **ANGIE** and **ANGEL** run into the space.)*

ANGIE. Hey Mews!

ANGEL. Mewwwwwws!

MEWS. Hey.

ANGIE. You wouldn't happen to have seen two newbies walking around?

ANGEL. They were supposed to be following us through the trails but we lost them.

MEWS. Did they know you'd be running?

ANGIE. Angel bet me that I couldn't beat him on the trail.

ANGEL. I was a cross country phenom.

MEWS. Who won?

ANGEL. *(Defeated.)* She did.

> (**ANGIE** *shows off her bag of Sour Patch Kids.*)

ANGIE. Don't tell the DieKayKay we //

> (**BENJAMIN** *enters.*)

BENJAMIN. Don't tell me what?

ANGIE. What?

ANGEL. What?!

> (**ANGIE** *and* **ANGEL** *quickly exit.*)

BENJAMIN. I swear those two get stranger every time.

MEWS. Maybe this place does something to them.

BENJAMIN. Did you know that there are five hundred and three species of birds in New York state alone?

MEWS. Umm?

BENJAMIN. Birds tend to be a symbol of freedom because of their ability to fly. Go wherever they want to go. But raise a bird in a cage, even if you let it out, leave the cage door open the odds are that bird will come back to that cage every time. The cage is familiar. Comfort over freedom.

MEWS. I feel like there's a message?

BENJAMIN. You, Angel and Angie. Hopefully this time around we can get the program to stick. If I can do it you can. It doesn't work if you don't work it.

MEWS. I'm here, aren't I?

BENJAMIN. Are you?

Do me a favor. Keep an eye on Jasmine.

MEWS. Why?

BENJAMIN. I have a feeling.

See you tomorrow morning for group.

3. Poker Face

(We find ourselves in a room that resembles the quintessential dorm room. **JASMINE** *sits unpacking her things.* **GIANNA** *enters.)*

JASMINE. These rooms are bigger than I thought they'd be.

Hi. I'm Jasmine.

GIANNA. You're like really pretty.

JASMINE. Um...tha– thank you.

GIANNA. Have you met Mews?

JASMINE. Yeah briefly, earlier.

Why?

GIANNA. They broke up with me, it was a thing, it's not a thing anymore. It's whatever. My name's Gianna.

JASMINE. Got it.

GIANNA. I think they like that Bible-humpin' bitch.

JASMINE. Hey I don't mean this in a dismissive way but you're not crazy are you? I really don't want the crazy roommate.

GIANNA. We're all here because we have a hole inside us that we like try to fill with like the adrenaline rush of the possibilities of making the hole deeper and wider. We fill emptiness with emptiness.

JASMINE. I'm just trying to keep my head down and get my thirty days over without incident. Is that gonna be possible with you?

GIANNA. You have nothing to worry about from me.

JASMINE. Great.

You're pretty too.

GIANNA. Aww, you're sweet. Like this is my first time here but I know a lot of the kids that have gone here. From what I know, as long as you follow the rules, this place is a breeze.

JASMINE. Got it. The schedule says group therapy session is at 7:30 in the morning tomorrow?

GIANNA. Yep. You don't want to be late for that.

JASMINE. What do we use for an alarm without our phones?

GIANNA. That clock right there.

JASMINE. This?

This is something from my grandparents' era.

How do you even set it?

(**JASMINE** *fiddles with the alarm clock.*)

I think this is right.

I'm a heavy sleeper so if my alarm goes off and I don't get up just give me a shake.

GIANNA. I'd like rather not be responsible.

JASMINE. Kick the bed. Yell my name. That's it.

GIANNA. I don't know.

JASMINE. Gianna...

If I get kicked out of this program...

I can' t get kicked out of this program.

GIANNA. Why? You could just go somewhere else. There's like a facility in Saratoga that's supposed to be nice. It's in the same area as the casino out there which is like super silly but //

JASMINE. Just help me out.

GIANNA. I'll do my best.

JASMINE. Thank you. I can already tell Benjamin is going to be a pain in my ass.

GIANNA. DieKayKay is harmless.

JASMINE. What is that? DieKay– //

GIANNA. It's something Mews calls him. It's like an acronym. D Y K K

JASMINE. DYKK?

GIANNA. Did You Know Kid.

Once you hear it you'll get it.

JASMINE. If you say so.

Good night.

4. Tells

(In choreographed chaos the **CAST**, *except for* **JASMINE**, *set the chairs for the group therapy scene.* **THEO, ROXY, MARIE, MEWS, GIANNA, SERENITY, ANGEL, ANGIE** *and* **BENJAMIN** *sit in the chairs.* **BENJAMIN** *sits in the last stage right chair. There is one chair that sits empty.)*

BENJAMIN. Good morning, welcome to our first group session. Thank you for being on time as it is crucial for your journey towards a healthy balanced life that you prove to yourself that you can be reliable. As we always say, responsibility reinforces rehabilitation. Gianna, where is Jasmine?

GIANNA. I don't know.

BENJAMIN. You are roommates, correct?

*(***GIANNA** *shrugs.)*

THEO. If we had our PHONES you could just see our locations.

BENJAMIN. Did you know that the W.H.O. declared loneliness a significant global health threat? They say the mortality effects of loneliness are equivalent to smoking fifteen cigarettes a day.

THEO. I guess a bitch needs to get boo'd up ASAP. Mews what's your cute self doing tonight? It's a matter of life and death.

(Everyone laughs except **BENJAMIN** *and* **GIANNA**. **JASMINE** *enters and quickly takes her seat.)*

BENJAMIN. Jasmine, so glad you could join us.

JASMINE. Sorry, I overslept. My alarm didn't go off.

BENJAMIN. That's unfortunate and that's strike one.

JASMINE. What?! Why?

BENJAMIN. You were late. It clearly states in your Dos and Don'ts pamphlet that tardiness will not be accepted.

JASMINE. Come on! That's not fair!

I didn't set that stupid alarm clock right.

Don't do this to me.

BENJAMIN. I'm not doing anything to you. Your actions have consequences.

JASMINE. Oh my god!

SERENITY. Please don't use the Lord's name in vain.

JASMINE. Shut up!

BENJAMIN. Hey! Your behavior is warranting a second strike.

Don't let the cushy amenities fool you. This is a rehabilitation center not a resort. Your poor decisions and lack of discipline are what got you ALL here.

(*A moment.*)

Okay. Now let's get started.

JASMINE. (*To* **GIANNA.**) Thanks for waking me up roomie.

(**GIANNA** *gives her the Kanye shrug.*)

THEO. Oop! Shade.

BENJAMIN. Since this is our first day I'd love it if you all just briefly introduce yourselves and share what brought you here.

Jasmine you start.

JASMINE. I don't want to.

BENJAMIN. Your inability to manage your wants is what got you here. Did you know that //

> (**JASMINE** *bitterly laughs.*)

JASMINE. Got it. DY Kay. Kay. You're the "Did you know" kid.

THEO. Ohhh.

BENJAMIN. Please don't call me that.

ANGEL. YES! Told you!

ANGIE. Damn!

BENJAMIN. Excuse me!

ANGIE & ANGEL. Sorry.

> (*A moment.* **ANGEL** *tosses* **ANGIE** *Sour Patch Kids.*)

THEO. I can go first.

BENJAMIN. Theo I'd much rather //

THEO. It's fine.

> (**THEO** *stands up.*)

Hi I'm Theo.

> (*A moment.*)

Aren't y'all supposed to say "Hi Theo"?

> (*Silence.*)

BENJAMIN. It's not necessary. Go ahead.

THEO. Well that was disappointing.

I'm here because my addiction led me to losing ten thousand dollars in one month.

> (*Everyone in the* **CAST** *laughs except for* **JASMINE** *and* **MEWS**.)

ROXY. That's it? I spend that amount on a regular Tuesday.

MARIE. We have clutch bags worth four times that.

ANGEL. My minimum bets start at ten g's.

ANGIE. You sure you should be here? You might want to go to the beginners level rehab. Is there such a thing?

BENJAMIN. Okay. Alright. Enough.

THEO. Cute.

As I was saying, I'm here because I lost ten thousand dollars in one month playing Candy Crush.

(The room erupts in shock, awe and disbelief.)

BENJAMIN. Okay, calm down everyone.

THEO. See exactly. Y'all thought I was basic. No hunty, my family is well off and I am well taken care of. There's no way I could afford this luxury rehab center otherwise. What's it like eighty grand a month?

GIANNA. You could've been one of those State babies.

THEO. Eww, no. I can pay my own way. Thank you.

ANGIE.	ANGEL.
State babies!	State babies!

BENJAMIN. Let's refocus people.

So you've shared the what. Now share the why.

THEO. I mean I hate to lose and the game, all those games are made to be addictive. Right? Okay. Umm.

You were saying before about loneliness being a health hazard or whatever. And it got me thinking about how lonely my existence has been. I mean with the money my family has and the schools they've sent me to, I'm almost always the only brown face in the room. And it's whatever, I make do, but I've never really felt like I fit anywhere, belonged anywhere you know? And the games on my phone were always this escape this safe place that I could, I dunno, feel special? Making it to the next level just made me feel special //

BENJAMIN. Thank you Theo.

Community is so important and a key factor to healthy living with your addictions.

ROXY. We got a better story than that.

MARIE. Sure do.

BENJAMIN. Well it's not a //

SERENITY. What Theo shared was deep but I feel like mine is deeper.

BENJAMIN. We're not //

ANGIE. Wanna bet?!

> (*A game buzz sounds, lights change and we're thrust into a hyperrealistic world of personal sharing. They are competing for the best story.*)

ROXY. Dancing was the one thing we loved to do.

MARIE. Our mother made us give it up because –

ROXY. "There is no financial future in dancing."

MARIE. And she made us take private business lessons with this tutor

ROXY. So annoying but then watching our favorite movie of ALL Time

MARIE. *You Got Served!*

ROXY. We started our own high-stakes dance competition. It was amazing.

MARIE. Until this kid got shot. Kinda like in the movie, which was cool but not. You know? Tragic.

ROXY. Tragic.

>   *(...)*

GIANNA. After the divorce, when it was my father's time
to have me, From like six years old to twelve my father
would drop me off at Dave & Busters, give me his credit
card and leave me there alone the entire day. No one
should be as good at Skee-Ball as I am!

>   *(...)*

ANGEL. I am the greatest fantasy football player in the
world!

ANGIE. Excuse me?

ANGEL. I am the second greatest fantasy football player in
the world!

>   *(...)*

SERENITY. My nanna loved to play Bingo. I would always
play with her when I visited her in the nursing home.
We would talk for hours, mostly about how lonely she
was and then one day while playing Bingo God called
her home. I was right there next to her. I think I was six
years old?

>   *(...)*

MEWS. We were raised Catholic and well...

I spell my name M E W S because as a kid Mew was
my favorite Pokémon character. Its DNA combines the
genetic composition of all existing Pokémon species,
and even when I was young I was like, "yeah that's me."
I'm all things. Let's just say Catholic school didn't agree
with me. I learned to have a poker face earlier on.

>   *(...)*

THEO. I have carpal tunnel syndrome! I am too young for this. But my parents let the tablets and phones be my babysitter so here we are. I have the grip of a hundred-year-old in hospice.

> (...)

> (The **CHARACTERS** *combine in a cacophony of one upping gibberish until game buzzer sounds.*)

JASMINE. FINE I'LL SHARE NOW.

> (*We return to normalcy.*)

BENJAMIN. Well that's our time for today. Thank you all for sharing. You can find your chore assignments for today on the bulletin board in the Mess Hall. Remember. Responsibility reinforces rehabilitation.

> (**BENJAMIN** *exits.*)

THEO. O. Kay.

Are we cured yet?

JASMINE. What is Benjamin's deal? He's not much older than us. Seriously who put him in charge?

MEWS. Benjamin was a child prodigy.

Second youngest to graduate college at the age of eleven. Got his Master's at fourteen and at fifteen fell in love with poker. He traveled the world and won a bunch of money but always came home looking so sad. He checked himself into rehab got another Master's in psychology and never looked back.

THEO. Wait, came home?

MEWS. Benjamin's my older brother.

THEO. Isn't you being here like a conflict of interest or something?

MEWS. Our parents wouldn't have it any other way.

ANGIE. Yo! I DO KNOW YOU! Jasmine Bythewood.

ANGEL. We lost thirty racks because of you.

ROXY. What's happening?

MARIE. Who is she?

ANGIE. Don't you watch the news? She started her own app that had like almost half of all the high schools in the tri-state area betting on high school basketball games.

MEWS. Oh wow. I do remember this. That's you?

ANGIE. Before they caught you you had like millions.

So we have a pool going on who we think will get kicked out of here first. You want in?

JASMINE. That's against the rules. No thanks.

GIANNA. Why don't you just take a picture of her Mews? It'll like last longer!

(**GIANNA** *storms out.*)

ANGIE. Drama

ANGEL. Draaama!

ANGIE & ANGEL. DRAMA!!

ANGIE. You sure you don't want to get in on this bet?

JASMINE. Get away from me.

ANGEL. Away.

ANGIE. Away.

ANGIE & ANGEL. AWAY!

(**ANGIE** *and* **ANGEL** *exit.*)

THEO. We have to be here for twenty-nine more days with those weirdos.

ROXY. You really made millions with a betting app?

JASMINE. Yeah.

MARIE. How?

JASMINE. All you need is to Jailbreak your phone. Hop on the Dark Web and accept bitcoin bets only.

ROXY. How'd you get caught?

JASMINE. My story was on every major news outlet. Just google it.

MARIE. We don't have any internet access remember?

JASMINE. Can we circle back to Mews and Benjamin being siblings?

ROXY. That's old news.

MARIE. Yeah we've been known.

THEO. Since when?

ROXY. Yesterday, Gianna told us.

MARIE. Theo aren't you on kitchen duty with us?

THEO. I think so.

ROXY. We should go now, it takes like ten minutes to walk to the dining hall from here.

MARIE. We have to be there at nine sharp and it's eight forty-five.

THEO. Oo, I'm so glad y'all can read that analog, cause I definitely would've been late.

I'll see you later girl.

Bye Mews.

MARIE.	**ROXY**.
Bye Jasmine	Bye Mews

(The three of them exit.)

JASMINE. So?

MEWS. What?

JASMINE. What's the deal with your brother?

MEWS. He can be...sensitive when he feels threatened.

JASMINE. Threatened?

MEWS. Benjamin needs to be the smartest in the room. Always.

JASMINE. Why didn't you mention you two were //

MEWS. It's not a secret.

You wouldn't even tell me your name yesterday.

JASMINE. I didn't know you.

MEWS. I didn't know you either. That's the whole point of talking after you're introduced. To get to know the person.

JASMINE. Yeah well anyway I can also tell when someone's trying to activate the Rizz so

(**MEWS** *laughs as if caught red-handed.*)

MEWS. What? I was not.

JASMINE. You straight-up put on the flirtatious voice.

MEWS. That's just my voice.

JASMINE. Uh huh.

MEWS. There's a waterfall maybe a mile or so from here.

JASMINE. That's nice.

MEWS. You want to go and check it out?

JASMINE. Isn't it chore time? I can't get in trouble.

MEWS. You're with me. It's fine.

Come on.

JASMINE. I don't think so.

MEWS. I'll give you some Sour Patch Kids.

JASMINE. Why does everyone have Sour Patch Kids?

MEWS. The company that makes them invests in the GARY Center.

JASMINE. That's...something's wrong with that.

MEWS. Okay here's something nobody else knows. This facility is owned by our parents.

JASMINE. Are you serious?

MEWS. They built it when my brother was struggling with his addiction.

JASMINE. That's...why are you here?

MEWS. I mean, they also own two casinos so...it's in my blood.

Come on. You're safe with me.

JASMINE. There's that rizz-tainted voice of yours.

> *(They hold out their hand.* **JASMINE** *takes it and they exit. Transition to Jasmine and Gianna's room.* **GIANNA** *sits looking in her compact mirror.* **JASMINE** *enters.)*

GIANNA. We fill emptiness with emptiness.

JASMINE. It's really messed up that you didn't wake me up this morning. What's up with that?

GIANNA. Pretty girl like you. You'll figure it out.

JASMINE. Figure what out?

GIANNA. Life. Life like works out for those with desire on their side. It doesn't abandon you. That's why I don't feel bad for you.

JASMINE. Nobody asked you to feel anything for me.

GIANNA. Those red shirts in the corner are yours. Oh and Benjamin told me to tell you to come to his office. It's located in Building number three.

JASMINE. What for?

> (**GIANNA** *gives the Kanye shrug.* **JASMINE** *exits.*)

5. The House Always Wins

(**BENJAMIN** *stands in his office looking out his window.* **JASMINE** *tentatively enters.*)

JASMINE. Benjamin? Gianna said you wanted to see me?

(**BENJAMIN** *turns. Takes her in for a second and then turns back to look out of the window.*)

BENJAMIN. Did you know that in 2008 UNLV did a study that showed that online gambling was more addictive than casino gambling? Then five short years later, New Jersey, Delaware and Nevada became the first states to legalize online gambling. Then four more states joined a few years after that and through lobbying and legislation soon all fifty states will be onboard. Money is and will always be the thing that we value over human life. I learned that lesson at a young age. Probably too young. But here we are.

JASMINE. Um. Where are we?

BENJAMIN. You missed your chores. That's strike two.

JASMINE. I was with your sibling. I was with Mews.

BENJAMIN. And you went for a hike right?

JASMINE. Yes. They showed me the waterfall. They said it would be okay. I know about your parents.

BENJAMIN. Is that what you wore on your hike?

JASMINE. What? Yes.

BENJAMIN. It clearly states in your manual, when you go on hikes you are required to wear the facility's red shirts.

That's strike three.

JASMINE. Are you serious?! No! No!

BENJAMIN. I already called for a shuttle to take you back to the city. I'll notify your parole officer and the state tomorrow morning.

JASMINE. Benjamin please!

Mews said it would be okay. They said.

BENJAMIN. Mews is an addict with no impulse control. Why would you trust them? The reality is you were never going to make all thirty days so better sooner than later.

> (**JASMINE** *storms out. Transition to the Mess Hall where* **THEO, MARIE** *and* **ROXY** *are working on a new dance routine.* **SERENITY** *is reading her Bible.* **MEWS** *is staring at* **SERENITY. GIANNA** *is starting at* **MEWS.**)

6. Ante Up

MEWS. My Aunt tells me all the time I'm going to hell. Do you think I'm going to hell?

SERENITY. One can only pray.

JASMINE. *(Offstage.)* MEWS!!

> (**JASMINE** *storms into the room.*)

You said I'd be okay?!

MEWS. What?

THEO. What's happening? What's wrong?

JASMINE. I'm getting kicked out.

THEO. Why?

JASMINE. Because I trusted this piece of shit.

SERENITY. Language.

MEWS. I didn't do anything.

JASMINE. Well do something now. Tell your brother not to kick me out.

MEWS. He can be stubborn but I'll try.

GIANNA. You want the number to the, like, facility in Saratoga?

ROXY. Yeah why you so worked up? Just go somewhere else.

MARIE. The one in Saratoga is near a casino, so that's cool right?

JASMINE. I can't do that?

ROXY. Why not?

JASMINE. I'm not privileged like you all here. I'm a, what did you say Gianna? A "State Baby." I need this program to stay outta jail. If I don't complete the thirty days I've "wasted" the State's money and that is punishable with jail time. Incentive right? So that us poor folk don't take advantage of the system right? But is what I have, this addiction, a disease or nah? Is society responsible or nah? The bombardment of casinos, online games, fantasy this, draft kings that, scratch offs, mega millions, in-game purchases, clickbait, scroll up, scroll down, swipe left, swipe right, like like like like like.

I have a five-year-old brother that I'm going to have to take care of. Our father died overseas; Mom's dying of breast cancer //

GIANNA. So you're like basically on welfare?

JASMINE. What is your problem?!

MEWS. Okay let's enhance our calm.

THEO. Mews you have to talk to Benjamin for her.

(*ANGEL and ANGIE enter.*)

ANGIE. What's up fellow addicts?

ROXY. Jasmine's getting kicked out.

ANGEL. Oh no!

ANGIE. Dammit!

Okay everyone ante up.

(**ANGEL, ANGIE, GIANNA, ROXY, MARIE** *and* **MEWS** *all give* **SERENITY** *a bag of Sour Patch Kids.*)

THEO. What's happening?

MARIE. Serenity called it.

ROXY. How'd you know?

SERENITY. When the almighty speaks to me I listen.

MARIE. I thought it would be you Theo.

ROXY. Me too.

THEO. What the hell?

MARIE. I mean Jasmine had more of an attitude but you're way more hood.

ROXY. Way more hood.

GIANNA. I thought Theo too.

THEO. Oh my...okay that's... Jasmine eff these people.

(**THEO** *exits.* **BENJAMIN** *enters.*)

BENJAMIN. Jasmine you should really get going the shuttle will be here for you soon.

JASMINE. Mews.

MEWS. Bro, can't you give Jasmine another chance. It's kinda my fault.

JASMINE. Kinda?!

BENJAMIN. Actions have consequences. You should both know that by now.

JASMINE. You're a coward. You can act all healed when there's literally nothing here to tempt you. You've isolated yourself out here. No communication. No real technology. What do you have to lose? What do any of you have to lose? Life is just one big game huh? You know what. Forget it.

(**JASMINE** *exits.*)

BENJAMIN. Our facility gets the state funding your body provides whether or not you complete your thirty days. You've served your purpose!

(*A moment. The other* **CHARACTERS** *just look at* **BENJAMIN.**)

What?

Come on we have our sensory deprivation tank sessions in fifteen minutes.

7. Folding

(Nature sounds fill the space. The wind rustling leaves, a far off waterfall gently rumbles. **JASMINE** *stands waiting for her shuttle.* **THEO** *enters with his rolling suitcase.)*

THEO. Jasmine, girl. Are you okay?

JASMINE. Theo what are you doing?

THEO. I'm coming with you.

JASMINE. What? No. Why?

THEO. I'm not staying out here with these privileged ass folk. I mean I come from some privilege but I'm clear on the intersections. I've seen enough horror movies to know if you're not here I'm next to be killed. No thank you.

JASMINE. Don't mess up your rehab for me.

THEO. Ain't nobody messing nothing. I'm supposed to be out here to get rid of my toxic behavior. How am I supposed to do that here? Girl I should have done better research when I choose this place. All these trust fund and nepo babies and not one celebrity. So disappointing.

They have to have a facility out there that's specifically for black and brown folk right?

JASMINE. Yeah it's called prison.

THEO. Damn.

(A moment.)

Hey, it's going to be okay. My parents have some political connections. We can ask them for help when we get back.

JASMINE. Theo I don't...

THEO. Shh! Listen. What's the point of going to rehab if
you not gonna come out with connections?

We got six hours on this triflin' ass shuttle. We'll figure
it out.

   (A moment.)

JASMINE. I can't believe they thought *you* were hood.

THEO. Girl!

End of Play

Milewalkers

by Jesús I. Valles

MILEWALKERS premiered with Keen Company (Jonathan Silverstein, Artistic Director) as part of the Keen Teens Festival of New Work at Theatre Row in New York City on May 17, 2024. The performance was directed by Jean Carlo Yunén, with sets by Yi-Hsuan (Ant) Ma and Yun Yen, costumes by Dan Wang, lights by Hayley Garcia Parnell, sound by Eden Segbefia, and props by Caitlyn Murphy. The Production Stage Manager was Sloane Fischer. The cast was as follows:

FAHREN	Bianca Vigilante
ALYSSA	Kiera O'Grady-Chabrán
SONIA	Ariana Peña
COACH DUARTE	Ryan Tan
SAVANNAH	Amirah Clark
OSCAR	Jermaine Birchett
LUIS	Dereck Diller
ERIC	Xavier Frank
DAVID	Max Lobis-Green
MAURI	Angelina Gomez

CHARACTERS

(Inhabit them as you will; gift the heart – invite the full of yourself to playing them.)

FAHREN – she/her, 8th grade, Monroe piercing, decisive, brutal. Will absolutely beat you in a fight, will absolutely join any fight you are in.

ALYSSA – she/her, 8th grade, perfect eye makeup, loyal, romantic. Will absolutely listen to all your problems, will absolutely tell you all of hers.

SONIA – she/her, 8th grade, she's new here, brand-new, observant, dedicated. Will absolutely help you with your work, but won't let you copy. Will absolutely lie to a teacher for you. NOTE: this actor should be able to play an older version of **SONIA**, too.

COACH DUARTE – he/him, P.E. Coach, so he's a P.E. coach, deeply self-serious. Flopped jock energy.

SAVANNAH – she/her, 8th grade (should be in 9th), powerful, charming, hungry, older cousin energy, thinking about mortality and illness a lot, raised by her grandma. Will absolutely reply with "That's crazy" to everything, whether she's listening to you or not.

OSCAR – he/him, 7th grade, gayby, quiet, going through it, sweet, sentimental, deeply apologetic. Should ideally be the smallest person onstage, and with a tremendous amount of heart. NOTE: this actor should be able to play an older version of **OSCAR**, too.

LUIS – he/him, 8th grade, runs track, rude. A mean, bro-code kind of athlete-archetype, fairly antagonistic. Ideally should look like he could run track, but then again, it's middle school.

ERIC – he/him, 8th grade, runs track, trying really hard to sound like he has a deeper voice, is forever nervous that he might not be good enough, Oscar's cousin, so some relation.

DAVID – he/him, 8th grade, runs track, too tall to know what he's doing, Alyssa's crush, Oscar's crush, too. Not too many words out of him.

MAURI – they/them, 7th grade, too young but already a queer elder, so very willfully themselves, loves tarot and is very likely deep in witch-Tok. If middle school had case workers, they would be first in line for the job.

SETTING

Hillcrest Middle School's courtyard/field/track. Texas.

TIME

Fall semester of some school year between 2004 and 2019,
but maybe now, too. Milewalkers are eternal.

AUTHOR'S NOTES

A Note on Language
I invite you to play with the texture of the language for specificity
and, obviously, to adjust the curse words if it feels necessary for your
production. I only ask that you contact your Licensing Representative at
Concord Theatricals prior to doing so for productions, but I'm happy to
work with your team in this regard.

Also, the dialogue should at times feel like overlapping, like conversation
might, so, when you see a "/", the next line of dialogue should come in.
Where a forward slash interrupts a character's dialogue and is followed
by stage directions, the stage direction should be the cause of the
interruption.

The Rules
Play it fast.
Think less, know more.
Say the words how you best want to say them.
Play. Eat. Move.
It's Texas in August/September, so it's hot.

(Morning. It's Wellness Wednesday [but it's on a Thursday today, cuz of the holiday] at Hillcrest Middle School. Outside, in the courtyard, **FAHREN** *and* **ALYSSA** *flank* **SONIA**. **ALYSSA** *is holding a Ziplock bag with ice, holding ice to* **SONIA**'s *ear. It's preparation for a rite of passage.)*

SONIA. Ffffffffff... Oh my god. It's so cold, it's so / cold

ALYSSA. It's ice, stupid. You want it to be warmer? / It's supposed to be cold.

SONIA. It kinda hurts. You know when it's cold and it burns? That's – How long does / it have to –

FAHREN. Just till you can't feel your ear, so it's numb –

> *(**FAHREN** pulls a safety pin and a lighter from her pocket, along with two little alcohol pads. She heats the pointy part of the pin.)*

...when the pin goes through. Can feel your ear / right now –

SONIA. You're gonna do it with a safety pin?! That's...

I don't think that's safe. / I don't –

FAHREN. That's why I'm disinfecting the safety pin, so you don't get sick, okay?! Calm down! Trust me, I've done this a lot. *(She indicates the piercings on her cartilage and her lobes.)* I did these, see? / I'm fine.

SONIA. *(To **FAHREN**.)* Who else have you done this for?

FAHREN. Uh... I did Oktavea, and me, and I did Eric's, too. / Okay, almost there –

SONIA. Eric...?

FAHREN. *(She turns out to shout at* **ERIC**, *who is off, away.)*
ERIC! EY! DUDE! EY ERIC!

> *(He turns.)*

NOTHING! TURN AROUND! DON'T BE LOOKING
AT ME, MENSO! UGH!

(To **SONIA**.*)* That Eric.

SONIA. But he doesn't have an earring...?

FAHREN. Yeah, he got an infection and it closed up. Okay,
Alyssa, / check her ear.

> (**ALYSSA** *pinches* **SONIA**'s *ear where the ice
> has been.* **SONIA** *winces. It's time.)*

SONIA. Wait – / Ah ah –

ALYSSA. Did you feel it?

SONIA. Kinda, yeah

FAHREN. Cool. You should be good, though *(To* **ALYSSA**.*)*
Hold her.

(To **SONIA**.*)* It'll be quick.

ALYSSA. She did my ears, too, and I didn't get sick.

You got really pretty eyes. You should wear eyeliner. /
She's got pretty eyes, huh?

SONIA. *(To* **ALYSSA**.*)* Thanks. My dad doesn't let me wear
eyeliner, though. Maybe in high school *(The safety pin
goes through and –)* / – AHHHH!!!

> (**FAHREN** *pierces* **SONIA**. *A spectacular
> amount of blood. So much blood. That's
> crazy.)*

AHHHH! OH MY GOD! OH MY GOD! AHHH! /
WHAT THE F–

(From off, away, in the distance.)

COACH DUARTE. Alright, guys, make sure everyone's suited out. Let's huddle up! LET'S GO! LET'S GO! LET'S GO! / HUSTLE! HUSTLE! HUSTLE!

> *(**COACH DUARTE** blows his whistle! **SONIA** steps out for a moment. Time slows behind her. Debussy's "Clair de Lune."* * *She's with us now, years later, at thirty. Middle school plays behind her. The **GIRLS** are there, then.)*

SONIA. This is how I remember them best. This version of them right here. Feral. Fearless.

This is the first time I think I ever felt loved by people who weren't family.

Hi. Yes, this is a memory play now, sort of.

> *(**FAHREN** and **ALYSSA** argue in the back about the piercing, slowly, inaudible.)*

Mostly it's a symptom of longing. It's a memory. I miss them so much, now that I'm older. They were the reason I understood my aunties, why they were like that with each other. So mean. So close. I understood why my mom and her friends were so tight.

> *(**FAHREN** and **ALYSSA** start to shove each other. Maybe they punch each other. Maybe **FAHREN** bites **ALYSSA**'s arm. It's sweet. They laugh.)*

It was the first time I felt how brutal and caring we could be with one another. They were so free.

That...piercing hurt so much. Bless them.

---

* A license to produce *Milewalkers* does not include a performance license for any third-party or copyrighted recordings. Licensees should create their own.

SONIA. When I walk into a gas station or a corner store on a weekday and see girls skipping class,

I think about them. I get pulled back there.

> *(She gets pulled back then.* **SONIA** *is back there again with* **ALYSSA** *and* **FAHREN**. *Time resumes.* **COACH** *blows his whistle.)*

AHHH!!! THAT HURT! YOU SAID IT / WOULDN'T HURT –

ALYSSA. "HuStLe! HuStlE!" He's so annoying, / I swear

FAHREN. Shut up! Shut up! It didn't hurt that much! It's done! It's done!

> *(She takes an alcohol wipe and cleans* **SONIA***'s ear.)*

Okay, / I'm just gonna disinfect your –

ALYSSA. Oh my god, she's so dramatic! You're so dramatic! You didn't even bleed that much, / anyway.

You swear –

FAHREN. Where's the earring?

> *(***SONIA*** hands ***FAHREN*** the earring. It's been in her palm the whole time.)*

Okay, I'm / just gonna put it –

ALYSSA. Amethyst! That's amethyst, huh? You're a Pisces, or what? Yeah, you're a Pisces, huh?

That's why you cry a lot. I'm a Cancer, so I could just kinda / feel it, y'know?

SONIA. Aquarius. February, though. Hey, I think the cold wore off, it's really / starting to hurt –

FAHREN. It's fine! Just put alcohol on it at night and don't take out the earring for a while / so that it doesn't –

ALYSSA. Oh, Aquarius. Yeah, I knew it. I could see it. Dude, it looks kinda swollen. Are you like, allergic to metal and stuff / or, like what? Cuz –

FAHREN. Okay, let's do the other side. Put the ice / on the other ear –

SONIA. No, I think I'm just gonna do this one today. I'm / gonna wait –

FAHREN. No, dude, cuz then you're gonna look like a pirate. Alyssa / get the other –

ALYSSA. Oh my god, a pirate –

> (*She spots* **COACH DUARTE**.)

/ Coach is coming Coach is coming Coach is coming! Put your stuff away.

SONIA. It's, like, throbbing. I can feel my heartbeat on / it. Is that normal?

FAHREN. Let me see. (*It's not normal.*) Oh, damn. / It's normal! It's fresh, you're good. Alyssa, give me the ice baggie.

SONIA. What? What?! What do you mean "Oh, damn." What does it look like? / Wait, is it –

> (**FAHREN** *puts her "piercing kit" in her drawstring bag.* **ALYSSA** *and* **SONIA** *try to look normal. They don't.* **COACH DUARTE** *enters, running up as all the other* **STUDENTS** *start to cluster near* **FAHREN**, **ALYSSA**, *and* **SONIA**.)

COACH DUARTE. YOU SHOULD ALL BE SUITED OUT NOW! LET'S GO! LET'S GO! LET'S GO! COME ON GUYS! (*To* **SONIA**.) You're new. I don't know you.

SONIA. Yeah, I just –

I got my schedule changed

(She hands him a crumpled up schedule.)

COACH DUARTE. *(Not even looking at her, watching for everybody gathering.)* Okay, yeah, yeah, that's good, man.

That's good. COME ON, GUYS! YOU RUN LIKE / MY GRANDMA!

ALYSSA. *(To **FAHREN**.)* He's so loud, / Oh my god –

FAHREN. So annoying. / Swear –

COACH DUARTE. LADIES! NO TALKING!

LUIS! DAVID! ERIC! HUSTLE! LET'S GO!

> *(**COACH** notices **SONIA**'s ear briefly. He hardly cares.)*

What's wrong with your ear? You bleeding?

SONIA. No.

COACH DUARTE. That's good, man.

COMEEEEE!! ON!!!!!

> *(**LUIS**, **DAVID**, and **ERIC** run up with precision. They apologize for their delay in unison.)*

LUIS, DAVID & ERIC. Sorry, sir. It won't happen again, sir.

ERIC. We got held back because / we were –

COACH. I DON'T WANNA HEAR IT! EXCUSES ARE LIKE BUTTS!

SONIA. *(To the **ALYSSA**.)* What did he say?

> *(Every **STUDENT** is gathered in their P.E. outfits now: athletic shorts, or basketball gear, or cartoon character-print pajama pants and a matching little drawstring bag, or or or – so many looks. The **STUDENTS** chatter about*

whatever. **COACH DUARTE** *blows his whistle!*
The talking continues.)

COACH DUARTE. Alright guys, listen up! Now, today's
gonna be / a very important day –

(*He blows his whistle.)*

ALYSSA. *(To* **FAHREN.***)* Dude, what's today? I don't / even
know –

COACH DUARTE. I SAID LISTEN UP! So, listen up!
I don't wanna write anybody up today.

So, are you guys gonna listen or what?

(Nothing.)

YOU GUYS GONNA LISTEN OR WHAT?

EVERYONE. *(With varying degrees of enthusiasm.)* Yeah.

COACH DUARTE. YESSIR! YOU GUYS SAY YESSIR!

EVERYONE. *(Even less invested in this.)* Yessir.

COACH DUARTE. OKAY, THAT'S MORE LIKE IT!
Alright guys, now look, I know most of you aren't used
to running. Getting soft, all day on your phones, on
your iPads, on TikToks / but tod–

FAHREN. Oh my god, he / swears –

COACH DUARTE. What's that, Fahren? / Huh?

FAHREN. Nothing.

COACH DUARTE. Yeah, that's right nothing. / Yeah.

FAHREN. Yeah. No-thing, sirrrR.

COACH DUARTE. Alright, that's enough, Fahren. I don't
wanna see you again next year / in here –

FAHREN. *(Through her teeth.)* I don't wanna see you
either. / Shit –

COACH DUARTE. *(Trying to drown her out.)* NOW! YOU GUYS have had ALL summer to just sit around and do nothing, but that's not what this class is about, guys, alright? ALRIGHT?! This is about how strong MINDS make – WHAT? About how strong MINDS make WHAT?!

LUIS, DAVID & ERIC. STRONG MINDS MAKE STRONGER BODIES, SIR!

COACH DUARTE. THAT'S RIGHT! And the only way to have a stronger mind is to be in shape. So, today, we're gonna start easy. We're gonna start with a walk, IF YOU WANT, alright? IF YOU WANT, you're gonna start off with a walk / just to warm up –

*(In a whisper, **MAURI** urges **OSCAR**.)*

MAURI. Oh my god. Gurl, just give him the note / now.

*(**OSCAR** raises his hand. He hesitates.)*

OSCAR. Mister

Mister

/ Mister...um

Mister

COACH DUARTE. COACH! Call me Coach. What's / up, guy?

OSCAR. Okay, sorry, mister.

Coach, my mom said I can't really do a lot today cuz I have an ear infection. Also, I had a concussion last semester, so I / um I have a...uh I –

I have a note from my doctor –

*(**COACH** laughs and laughs.)*

COACH DUARTE. You're not running with your ears, son, you're running with your legs, so I / need you to toughen up –

OSCAR. It's cuz of a balance problem. The note says cuz my ear infection – it could cause balance problems, so I...um... / I could fall so the doctor said I should probably –

FAHREN. *(To* **ALYSSA** *and* **SONIA**, *in a loud whisper.)* You could fall cuz of your ears? / Is that real?

ALYSSA. I guess. *(She pushes* **SONIA**.*)* You better be careful, Sonia.

Oooh, spooky!

SONIA. Stop it. Fahren, / my ear feels –

COACH DUARTE. LADIES! Don't make me tell you again or you're gonna have to do thirty pushups EACH! And lunges! *(To* **OSCAR**.*)* Alright guy, let me see the note, then!

> *(**OSCAR** walks the note to* **COACH DUARTE**,
> *so the* **GIRLS** *really see him.)*

FAHREN. Oh my god. He's so little.

ALYSSA. Short king. / So cute.

COACH DUARTE. Which reminds me, if ANY of you have doctor's notes –

> *(**OSCAR** hands* **COACH** *the note.)*

(Reading to himself, muttering.) "...may not do high impact...previous injuries...if you have any questions..."

(To **OSCAR**.*)* Yeah, alright, man. Yeah, you can just walk. Anyway, if you have ANY DOCTOR'S NOTES LIKE THIS ONE!

> *(He holds it up in a violation of FERPA.)*

COACH DUARTE. YOU MAKE SURE YOU HAND IT TO ME BEFORE THE BELL RINGS! BEFOOOOORE the bell rings, so we don't waste our time.

Now, I'm gonna be running with you guys. I'm
modeling. I'm doing GRADUAL. RELEASE / WITH
YOU GUYS

ALYSSA. Ew. "Release." / Ew. Oh my god

FAHREN. "Modeling." All ugly / he swears –

LUIS. Stop interrupting Coach.

ERIC. Yeah, it's disrespectful. Could you guys / stop?

DAVID. Yeah.

SONIA. Fahren, does it look / infect–

COACH DUARTE. LADIES! I SAID! I'M GONNA START
OFF RUNNING.

LUIS! DAVID! ERIC!

You guys are gonna run with me, too, alright. I expect
more from you guys. You wanna make sure you go
straight into junior varsity or varsity when you guys get
to high school. DON'T EMBARRASS ME!

LUIS, DAVID & ERIC. Sir Yessir!

COACH DUARTE. Alright, now, everybody, the rest of you
can start off walking but I'm gonna blow this whistle
and when you hear it – *(He blows his whistle.)* – like
that? WHEN YOU HEAR IT! THEN YOU! RUN!
WE'RE DOING THE MILE TODAY, GUYS?! Yeah,
yeah, alright – let's do it!

ALRIGHT! GET SET! READY!

> *(**COACH DUARTE** blows his whistle and
> runs. **LUIS**, **DAVID**, and **ERIC** run after him.
> The other **STUDENTS**, including **OSCAR** and
> **MAURI**, walk fast, ahead. **SONIA** starts to jog,
> but **ALYSSA** and **FAHREN** hold her back.)*

FAHREN. Nah.

We don't do that.

ALYSSA. We don't run.

I'm not trying to sweat. My cut-crease actually came out good today. I'm not sweating / it off.

FAHREN. Oh my god! It does look good, dude! 'irala. She's la Kylie. / Ew, that's sick –

SONIA. Coach said we should / warm up –

FAHREN. He doesn't even care. I took P.E. with him last year, too, / and he –

ALYSSA. She failed it last year. She failed P.E. *(She laughs.)* That's dumb, huh? / Like, –

FAHREN. Man, shut up, Alyssa.

I didn't fail. He didn't pass me cuz he doesn't like me.

ALYSSA. Don't lie, Fahren! You never went to class. She never went to class. Don't lie! *(To **SONIA**.)* She like NE-VER went –

FAHREN. Okay, and?! Tell her why then!? Aver, tell her why I didn't go! Aver!

*(To **SONIA**.)* Cuz I was with her dumbass! Cuz you were being a chillona and a stalker / and I had to –

>   *(**MAURI** and **OSCAR** powerwalk by them.)*

MAURI. Gurl, go!

OSCAR. I can't!

>   *(**MAURI** and **OSCAR** look back and push through to speed past. They almost bump the **GIRLS**!)*

ALYSSA. *(After **MAURI** and **OSCAR**.)* HELLO! Be careful! You guys are so rude!

*(To **FAHREN**.)* You were the one who said we should ditch and see what was up with David. *(To **SONIA**.)* She was the one, dude. She was like, "You should see what's up with him?" And I was like, "Well, I guess." / You make it sound –

SONIA. You were stalking David? Like David-from-this-period David?

FAHREN. A stalker, dude. Crazy. Like, obsessed with David last year, following him around, had his whole class schedule memorized. She put little hearts and sparkles on his picture in the yearbook, / and everything.

ALYSSA. FIRST of all, I draw hearts and sparkles on all my friends. Second of all, We were going out! We were like actually together. Well, not really. Kinda –

> (**LUIS**, **DAVID**, *and* **ERIC** *run past the* **GIRLS**. **COACH DUARTE** *follows after them.*)

SONIA. That David?

FAHREN. YES HIM DAVID! HIIIMM!

She's so dumb, dude! He's so ugly. / So gross.

SONIA. You guys went out last year?

ALYSSA. Yeah, we were kinda talking / and then –

FAHREN. Did HE know that? Did HE know you guys were talking?

Cuz it didn't look like it to me!

(To **SONIA**.*)* She gets crazy about guys since, like, kindergarten.

She's, like, obsessed / with boys.

ALYSSA. WE WERE GOING OUT! We were going out!

He just didn't wanna tell anybody / because he –

FAHREN. *(To* **ALYSSA**.*)* He's so ugly, Alyssa! He literally looks like if you drew a person with your finger.

(To **SONIA**.*)* He's ugly, huh? Don't you think she could do better? / She could do better.

SONIA. I could see why you like him, / but I don't really –

FAHREN. Anyway, he had A lunch last year, when I had P.E. and Alyssa's crazy, so she was like, "Come with me to lunch so we can see what he's doing." Cuz he was just, like, not answering her texts. Like at all.

ALYSSA. He would answer! He would! Just like, after school, / so that he could –

FAHREN. He was ignoring you, stupid! Ugly-ass, Gumby-ass pendejo.

Anyway, I would ditch to come with her, so I would get to P.E. late or like I wouldn't go, so Coach failed me cuz he doesn't like me.

ALYSSA. Wait, dude, what's today?

SONIA. It's Thursday.

ALYSSA. Okay, see, that's crazy! I'm psychic, cuz I was like, "Today feels like Thursday," and it is.

(To **SONIA**.*)* You like anybody here? Oh my god!

The earring looks so cute on you! Amethyst is your color.

We should do the other side, though, / before the bell –

SONIA. I think I might just go get the other side at the mall. It's starting to hurt a little more. Are you sure it doesn't / look like it's –

> (**SAVANNAH** *enters. She catches up to the group, half-running. She's got a medical bracelet, a backpack, and a huge BBQ Mills cup full of iced tea.)*

SAVANNAH. Why are you guys walking so fast today? Damn. Dude, I had to go to the doctor this morning cuz I had a panic attack yesterday, like, last night, and my grandma was saying that's it's probably cuz I got bad blood pressure like she does, but I was telling her it's a panic attack cuz I was just like thinking all night, like, I was just there in bed, and I was like thinking, like "Damn, that's crazy that like, we're just, like, alive" and I was like, oh my god, what if I live to be really old, that's hard, y'know? and I was like, Damn, that's crazy, cuz my grandma's super old and she was like, "I'm so tired of living," and I was like, "If she's tired, imagine how tired I'm gonna be?" cuz I'm tired now, and then I was thinking like, "Oh my god. What if my grandma dies?" cuz I don't wanna live with my mom again, and I got so sad, so I started hyperventilating and I text my grandma, cuz she was in the living room, I was like "Are you okay?" and she was like "Yeah, are you okay?" and I was like "I think I'm having asthma" and she was like "you don't have asthma," so she gave me some NyQuil, and then she was like, "I'm taking you to the doctor in the morning," and the doctor said it was probably a panic attack and that I probably should take melatonin or something, and then we went to BBQ Mills, cuz I didn't eat nothing, this morning, cuz I was still nauseous from last night. That's crazy, huh?

(*She takes a sip from her huge iced tea.*)

You guys think, Coach is gonna count me tardy?

ALYSSA. He doesn't care. You know he doesn't care. Look at him.

(**COACH DUARTE** *runs by the* **GIRLS. LUIS,** **ERIC,** *and* **DAVID** *run in.*)

COACH DUARTE. COME ON! COME ON! FASTER! GET THOSE KNEES UP TO YOUR CHEST! LET'S GO!

(**LUIS, ERIC,** *and* **DAVID** *exaggerate the extensions of their knees. They pass* **COACH** *and he runs after them.*)

SAVANNAH. Why's he running?

ALYSSA. He's trying to "release."

SAVANNAH. Ew, what the / hell?

ALYSSA. That's what he said. He's "releasing" and modeling.

You got BBQ Mills?

SAVANNAH. Tsk, I just said. It's on the cup all big. You can't read?

(*To* **FAHREN.**) Bruh. She can't read. / Public education.

ALYSSA. I can read. / I'm just asking –

SAVANNAH. They messed up my order, so I got an extra breakfast taco. Y'all want it?

FAHREN. What kind?

SAVANNAH. Brisket.

>   (*She notices* **SONIA.**)

Who's that?

FAHREN. This is Sonia. I have her for yearbook.

She changed her schedule so she's in this period now for P.E. She's from Tucson.

SAVANNAH. (*To* **FAHREN.**) You're in yearbook? Since when?

FAHREN. I needed a fine arts credit, so I'm taking / it for that.

ALYSSA. Yearbook's an art? How's yearbook an art? / That's not an art.

SAVANNAH. That's what I'm saying! You shoulda just taken art with Mr. Andrews.

He doesn't even care if you go. He's sad cuz his wife left him or something, I dunno, so we don't do anything in his class.

Anyway, (*To* **SONIA.**) I'm Savannah.

SONIA. I'm Sonia. Hi. It's nice to / meet –

SAVANNAH. What's wrong with you ear? Is it bleeding?

> (**FAHREN** *grabs another alcohol wipe and swabs* **SONIA***'s ear.*)

FAHREN. No, it isn't. IT'S FINE! She's fine! Look!

SAVANNAH. Well, it looks crazy.

> (*She takes out her taco from her bag.*)

You guys want it or nah?

SONIA. No, thank / you.

ALYSSA. Yeah, I'll / take it.

> (**FAHREN** *snatches the taco.*)

FAHREN. Nah, she offered it to me / first, fea.

> (**COACH DUARTE** *runs back up to the* **GIRLS***. He runs in place while talking to* **SAVANNAH***.*)

COACH DUARTE. SAVANNAH! You're late! / Again!

SAVANNAH. I'm sorry, / Coach.

COACH DUARTE. Go suit out!

SAVANNAH. I forgot my P.E. clothes at home. I've going through a lot lately cuz my grandma's been really sick and I think my parents are splitting up, and I have asthma, probably, or probably, like depression, / I think, so I –

COACH DUARTE. Yeah, okay, just don't forget next time.

> (**COACH DUARTE** *runs away.*)

SONIA. ...Hey, um...

I'm sorry you're –

If you're going through a lot right now,

Like, / if you're –

SAVANNAH. Oh, I just made all that up.

I never suit out anyway. I'm good, though.

SONIA. Oh, good. Okay, / that's good.

SAVANNAH. I mean, my grandma is sick, probably, and my parents split up, like, when I was ten, but only cuz my dad died, so it's kinda true, so / it's whatever.

ALYSSA. Dude, don't jinx it with your grandma. I lied to Mr. Baisch in sixth grade that my grandma died, and then she died for real. I mean, like a year later, but still she died. / So, like don't –

FAHREN. *(To* **SAVANNAH**.*)* You still got tea left? Could I get some? I haven't drank / nothing today.

SAVANNAH. Tsk. Uhg, just don't finish it like last time.

(To **SONIA**.*)* Dude, don't ever share nothing with them / cuz –

FAHREN. Please, dude. I'm so thirsty! I'm / gonna die!

ALYSSA. Me too! Give me some!

> (**OSCAR** *and* **MAURI** *power-walk by them again, stressed.)*

For real, I'm gonna die, too. I'm dehydrating right now.

(She lays herself out on the ground.)

See? I'm dying, dude. Oh my god. I'm dying of thirst.

ALYSSA. Save me, please.

(To **OSCAR**.*)* Hey

Hey!

You think she should save me? I'm dying / of thirst. Helppp meeeee...

OSCAR. *(Nervous.)* Yeah, uh,

> I guess you should save her and stuff.

> Or like. Help her.

ALYSSA. See?

> *(To **OSCAR**.)* Dude, you're so little.

> Uh. Hello?

> You okay?

>> (**MAURI** *looks back behind them and warns* **OSCAR**.)

MAURI. They're coming now. You're gonna have to run, girl. Try.

OSCAR. Shit.

>> (**MAURI** *runs.* **OSCAR** *walks away fast, a trot. He's off.)*

SAVANNAH. Oh my god! Not the cussing!

> Sir, there's kids here! / I'm a child!

FAHREN. Alyssa, get up, nasty! Oh my god, you're giving me anxiety for real, / get up off the floor –

ALYSSA. IT'S. GRASS. It's probably cleaner than the cafeteria, and we eat in there. It's just / grass, Fahren. *(To **SONIA**.)* Dude, she swears –

FAHREN. PEOPLE COULDA STEPPED ON DOG SHIT AND STEPPED / ON THE GROUND! ALYSSA, GET UP, NASTY!

SAVANNAH. Fahren, shut up, you're stressing me out!

> Alyssa, get up, you look crazy!

> *(To **SONIA**.)* This is who you want to be friends with for real?

SONIA. *(She laughs.)* Yeah. Yeah, I'm pretty sure.

I mean, they're your friends, too?

SAVANNAH. They're not my friends. I'm their case manager.

SONIA. What?

SAVANNAH. Tsk. Nothing. It's a joke.

(She turns back and looks. To **ALYSSA**.*)*

Your boyfriend's coming.

*(***LUIS**, **DAVID**, *and* **ERIC** *almost run past – they stop, running in place, too.)*

LUIS. You guys better hustle. Coach said you're / gonna have to run today.

SAVANNAH. Ew. Who says "hustle"?/ That's weird.

FAHREN. Why are you talking to us?

LUIS. What?

FAHREN. Why? Are you talking. To US? Shouldn't YOU be running? Mind your own business!

SAVANNAH. Yeah, Mind your own / business, chismoso.

ERIC. Guys, let's go! / We're wasting time!

LUIS. I'm just saying, you guys should be running. I don't want you guys to get in trouble / with Coach.

ALYSSA. Coach doesn't even care. / We're fine.

FAHREN. Ey, David, are you gonna keep ignoring Alyssa, / or are you gonna actually say hi? Hello?

ALYSSA. Fahren, shut up, dude. It's fine / we're not even talking like that anymore –

FAHREN. No, it's not fine. He's right there. His little friend is clearly stopping to bug us / so why doesn't he –

SAVANNAH. Hijole, that's true, dude. She's got a point. / That's true.

ALYSSA. Fahren, ya, don't be starting / stuff –

DAVID. *(He doesn't look at **ALYSSA**.)* Hey Alyssa.

ALYSSA. Hey / David.

FAHREN. DON'T SAY HI TO HIM BACK, DESPERATE!

ALYSSA. FAHREN! / SHUT UP!

LUIS. *(He nods to **SONIA**.)* Hey, what's up? You're new, huh?

SONIA. Just in this class. But I came in seventh grade.

Well, but like almost at the end / of the year, so –

LUIS. Cool. What's your / name?

ERIC. What's wrong with her ear? Did you –

*(To **SONIA**.)* Oh, shit. Did Fahren pierce your ear? She pierced mine last year / and it got infected.

FAHREN. NOTHING'S WRONG WITH HER EAR!

*(She picks up a rock, and throws it at **ERIC**.)*

LEAVE US / ALONE!

*(**ERIC** dodges the rock. **LUIS** and **DAVID** get closer to him to protect him.)*

LUIS. We were just saying hi, so you don't get in trouble!

This why nobody likes you!

FAHREN. Yeah, and why doesn't anybody / like YOU?

Huh? Dumbass. GO!

LUIS. Whatever, at least I live in an actual house, / not in a trailer, like some –

ERIC. Luis, shut up! Come on guys, let's go! Coach's gonna make us run a mile / today before practice, if we don't –

FAHREN. LIKE SOME WHAT?! SAY IT! You're gonna say something, SAY IT, PUTO!

Yeah, y'all should go, / yeah, good.

DAVID. Bye, / Alyssa.

ALYSSA. *(Too into it. Embarassing.)* Bye –

FAHREN. Don't talk to her!

> *(The whistle blows.* **DAVID,** **LUIS,** *and* **ERIC** *run off.)*

SAVANNAH. *(To* **FAHREN.**) Wow. You're like, extra crazy today.

Here.

> *(She hands* **FAHREN** *the cup.)*

Don't drink it from the straw though, nasty.

SONIA. *(She turns to* **ALYSSA.**) So, you and David... You guys are still –

You're talking still?

ALYSSA. I don't know.

I think we might end up just being friends, maybe?

FAHREN. He like, ignored you for / like the whole semester –

ALYSSA. He's just going through stuff. He's messed up.

SAVANNAH. Yeah, maybe he's got like ADHD or something or like epilepsy or maybe someone in / his family died, or –

SONIA. I don't think ADHD makes you ignore people. I think that's more, like, about schoolwork / and stuff.

ALYSSA. That's what I'm saying! I think he just had a bunch of stuff going on. I don't think / that's bad –

FAHREN. Then he can just say that! But he didn't! What?! You're just supposed to guess? You're not psychic, dude.

SAVANNAH. I think she's psychic.

FAHREN. What?

SONIA. I get it. It's hard, for guys, to talk about stuff like that.

My brother was like that, he didn't really like talking about stuff.

He was just kinda quiet. A lot.

SAVANNAH. He go here? Your brother?

SONIA. No. Uh. No.

He lived with my dad, in Tucson.

With us.

Before I moved here with my mom.

SAVANNAH. He move, too?

SONIA. No, he – uh –

I dunno. Uh –

Don't be weird

I don't need any of y'all to be weird or like –

I dunno, like be worried or anything

Yeah, just don't worry about it, but like –

No, he, like

Uh – he – uh

He killed himself.

And so, yeah.

I dunno.

Maybe.

Maybe David's going through something tough like that.

Like, maybe he's having a hard time and he doesn't know what to say, or like, what to do or something.

SAVANNAH. ...

Damn.

That's crazy. I'm sorry.

I'm sorry for your loss and stuff.

ALYSSA. Yeah, my condolences to him.

FAHREN. Yeah...me too.

I'm sorry. / I don't know.

SONIA. It's okay.

Really, like, it's okay.

It's been like, almost two years.

It's why we / moved –

ALYSSA. ...

So... So you think...

You guys think that's why we don't talk as much?

That maybe David's sad like that?

SONIA. My brother made weird jokes sometimes. Or like, wouldn't leave his room at all sometimes. I dunno. Is he... Is David like that? Does he ever talk / like –

ALYSSA. Not really. I mean, not like more than usual, / like –

FAHREN. What do you mean not more than usual? You guys just talk like that, all normal?

Like, "Oh yeah, I'm gonna unalive myself maybe. What'd you have for lunch?"

ALYSSA. You guys never talk about that, with people – like just about like dying and stuff?

SAVANNAH.	**FAHREN.**	**SONIA.**
Yeah, all the time.	No, what the hell?	Not as much anymore, but yeah.

FAHREN. Damn, that's so depressing. What are y'all sad about?

SAVANNAH. You don't have to be sad about stuff to think about dying.

Like, that's what I was thinking about last night.

People die all the time and like sometimes they could be happy. It's just, like, part of life.

FAHREN. *(She hands the iced tea cup back to* **SAVANNAH.***)* That's not healthy for you.

SAVANNAH. Oh my god, dude. You drank all of it! / Damn!

ALYSSA. You didn't even share, either! I'm gonna die / for real!

FAHREN. Don't joke about that! Don't joke about dying, dude! That's / offensive!

ALYSSA. To WHO!? How's that offensive? To WHOMSTTT?!

FAHREN. *(She eyes* **SONIA.***)* To. People. Stupid.

(Silence.)

(Then, **SONIA** *laughs.)*

SONIA. I'm not offended! Calm down!

FAHREN. It's disrespectful!

SONIA. To who? The dead community?!

Yeah, Alyssa don't joke about being dead, that's offensive to dead people!

ALYSSA. I'm so sorry!

I want to apologize to uh –

To dead people everywhere.

First of all, my grandma

(**ALYSSA** *busts out laughing.*)

FAHREN. Oh my god, Alyssa! STOP IT, DUDE!

SONIA. *(Laughing now, too.)* Yeah, Alyssa, that's offensive to my dead brother! Please apologize!

FAHREN. It's not funny to joke about dead people!

ALYSSA. I think it's kinda funny. We joke a lot about my grandma.

SAVANNAH. My grandma clowns so hard on my dad all the time and he died when I was little.

SONIA. We don't really joke like that in my family.

About my brother. I wish we did, cuz then at least we'd talk about it, y'know?

SAVANNAH. Yeah, it's like, more awkward when you don't talk about it.

FAHREN. I don't even like to think about it. That's so selfish, when people do that.

ALYSSA. When they die?

FAHREN. When they kill themselves. *(To* **SONIA.***)* Sorry, no offense.

SONIA. None taken. I mean, I'm not the one who killed himself.

FAHREN. Oh my god, / stop.

SAVANNAH. *(Taking out a bag of Hot Fries from her bag.*)*
I like this chick. She's funny.

(To **SONIA**.*)* You're funny. You want Hot Fries?

SONIA. Yeah, I'll take some.

I'm so hungry.

FAHREN. Give me some, / too.

SAVANNAH. See? What I tell you? Greedy.

> *(She pours some Hot Fries into* **FAHREN***'s cupped hands.)*

Dude, fun fact: One time I was so hungry I had ate dog treats.

FAHREN. *(She busts out laughing.)* Bitch, what?! How's that a fun fact? / Like?

SAVANNAH. It's a fun fact! Like, not everybody's done / that.

SONIA. Yeah, that doesn't seem that fun, if you like HAD to / eat dog treats –

SAVANNAH. No, but it's like a fun fact, / cuz like –

ALYSSA. Do you guys ever think about like how you want to die?

SAVANNAH. Uh. Dude, I just told you! Last night I really thought I was gonna die!

SONIA. I wanna die at my wedding.

FAHREN. You guys are so sick, / I swear.

SAVANNAH. That's so romantical, dying at your wedding!? With the love of your life, like, right there?

---

* A license to produce *Milewalkers* does not include a license to publicly display any branded logos or trademarked images. Licensees must acquire rights for any logos and/or images or create their own.

ALYSSA. How would you die at your weeding, though?

SONIA. From happiness?

ALYSSA. SHUT. UP. Oh my god. That's so corny.

"HaPpInEsS" Shut up!

(She busts out laughing.)

You're stupid!

SAVANNAH. That's crazy. Imagine?!

*(To **FAHREN** and **ALYSSA**.)* Y'all want more Hot Fries?

*(**OSCAR** and **MAURI** walk up behind them, fast.)*

MAURI. What about death? Somebody die?

Are you guys / talking about someone who died?

FAHREN. AH! Don't do that! Don't come up behind people like / that? Nosy.

OSCAR. Sorry, we're not trying to be nosy. We're just trying to get away from those guys / back there.

MAURI. Could we run with you guys for the period, / you think?

FAHREN. We don't know you.

MAURI. I'm Mauri, and this is Oscar. There. So, could we run / with –

SAVANNAH. We don't run. I got a condition.

MAURI. Like a heart condition?

SAVANNAH. Nah.

Y'all want Hot Fries?

MAURI. No, thank you, I'm not doing carbs.

SAVANNAH. Yeah, me neither. Oh, / Fun Fact: One time –

ALYSSA. Dude, don't! It's not a fun fact / at all!

FAHREN. *(To* **OSCAR***.)* You're not supposed to be running either, huh? Cuz of your ear?

OSCAR. Yeah, I have an ear infection. Plus I got a concussion last year, so I don't think the doctor wants me to risk falling / again.

ALYSSA. You play football?

SAVANNAH. *(She laughs.)* Plays football where? Look at him! He's so little.

He don't play no football! / Come on!

ALYSSA. You don't know! He could! Maybe he did like Pee-Wee football, / or something –

MAURI. No, you're right. She's not football girlie.

SONIA. She who?

MAURI. *(They point at* **OSCAR***.)* She her.

SONIA. Oh, you're –?

OSCAR. No, he/him.

But yeah, I'm –

Yeah / Um

FAHREN. Oh my god! You're gay!?! / Awww, that's so cute! Oh my god!

OSCAR. I mean...

Yes, but like / maybe don't –

SAVANNAH. *(Singing.)*
BE WHOOO YOU AREEEE!

See? I told you. He don't play football! I told / y'all see –

ALYSSA. This is SO crazy. I had, like, a feeling that something LGBTQIA was gonna happen to us, and like, it's happening. / I'm telling you –

MAURI. Yeah, no football for the little lady. Like, he'd get killed. Immediately. On the spot. Homophobic. Anyway, can we run with y'all? The jocks keep chasing Oscar and making fun of him cuz she can't run and / cuz –

OSCAR. Eric's my cousin. He's always been like that. He's just worse with his friends. Like, way worse. Do you think we could / just –

MAURI. That's how he got that concussion / last year –

OSCAR. Shut up, Mauri. Don't tell / people.

No, no, no – just –

He and his friends were, like, playing around / and then –

FAHREN. Hell no, dude. No, that's bullying. That's like, family violence. You could take him to court. My aunt took my cousin / to court –

OSCAR. No no no no! No, it wasn't like bad bad. It's just him and his friends were, like, teasing me because I told Eric that I liked David and so / he told David –

SAVANNAH. Damn. Double-homicide. / Another pendeja –

ALYSSA. Like David-in-this-class David? The tall / one –

OSCAR. Yeah, that David. So, he told David and like, then they just kept making fun of me / and like, I dunno –

MAURI. They kept pushing him around and making fun of him and David and Luis ended up pushing him too hard. But Oscar was like, "No, that's just how he plays / or whatever." I could put a spell on them. If you want. I could do / like –

SAVANNAH. You do spells?

MAURI. Yeah. I read tarot, too.

SAVANNAH. Oh my god. That's scary. You should do me. I wanna know how I'm gonna die and stuff.

OSCAR. Anyway, I sorta just fell back and hit my head and so, so / yeah, that's just been that since –

MAURI. David kicked him when he fell. But then I guess he felt bad cuz he picked him up.

He couldn't come to school for like almost all of the end of school. It was annoying.

And they're still being assholes, this year, I guess. I'm telling you, we could do a spell on him. Does anybody have graveyard dirt?

OSCAR. Anyway, they're just making fun of me, because of the ear infection thing, so every time they run by they keep trying to throw me off, or make me run away, / or –

FAHREN. That's your boyfriend, Alyssa. That's who you're worried about this whole time, is some dick who picks on his own / cousin –

ALYSSA. He's not my boyfriend! And I didn't know.

FAHREN. Oh, so now he's NOT your boyfriend? / Okay.

ALYSSA. Shut up, Fahren.

(To **OSCAR**.*)* I'm really sorry. I didn't know he was / like that –

OSCAR. Oh. That's your boyfriend?

ALYSSA. No, not really, not anymore, / anyway –

OSCAR. I'm sorry. I didn't know he had a girlfriend / or like – Yeah, I'm sorry.

SAVANNAH. Don't apologize to her for liking her man. That's not your fault / if you –

ALYSSA. He's not my man!

Seriously, though. Don't apologize. I get it. Why you'd like him? / I get it.

FAHREN. Ugh. Those guys are such dicks. I'm telling you, I hope they fuckin' fall and break their necks.

SAVANNAH. That's his cousin, dude. Didn't you say you didn't wanna talk about death?

FAHREN. Well, I don't hope he dies or anything, I just hope he like, breaks his neck.

MAURI. I feel like people die from that. Anyway, that's what happened. Can we run with / y'all?

SONIA. We don't run.

MAURI. Okay, well, is it cool if we walk with y'all?

FAHREN.	**ALYSSA.**	**SONIA.**	**SAVANNAH.**
It's whatever, yeah.	Yeah, it's cool.	Of course it's cool	My feet hurt. I think I got sciatica.

OSCAR. Thank you guys, so much. / Thank you.

ALYSSA. What's sciatica? Is that like a / foot thing?

MAURI. So why were you guys talking / about death?

SAVANNAH. I dunno. It's like a back thing, I think. It messes up your / walking or something.

SONIA. We were saying about how you'd want to die? Like, if you could choose.

FAHREN. No, YOU guys were talking about that shit. I wasn't. I think that's weird. / Like why –

OSCAR. That is really weird, honestly. Why are you thinking / about it?

MAURI. Would you guys rather burn to death or drown?

SAVANNAH.	**ALYSSA.**	**FAHREN.**
Drown.	I think I'd	NEITHER!
For sure.	rather burn?	The fuck?
I'd rather drown.	I think the	That's awful.
	smoke kills	
	you first.	
	So you don't	
	actually feel it.	

SONIA. Drown. Maybe.

Would you rather get hit by a bus or choke on a pretzel?

ALYSSA.	**SAVANNAH.**	**MAURI.**
Get hit by a bus!	What kind of	Pretzel... Wait?
Make it quick!	pretzel is it? That	
	would make a	...
	difference. Like if	
	it's a soft pretzel,	Bus? Maybe,
	yeah But not like	but what if it
	a hard one. That	takes too long?
	would suck.	Y'know? Like
		what if you get
		hit, but you
		just break your
		bones. It's giving
		very much
		Regina George.

SONIA. I choked on a Dorito one time.

I really thought I was gonna die. It was so painful.

Maybe the bus?

FAHREN. I hate this. I hate y'all so much. / I swear –

OSCAR. This is a really weird conversation. Could we talk about something else –

> (**COACH DUARTE** *blows his whistle. It's time to run. From off, away, he commands:*)

COACH DUARTE. LET'S GO! HUSTLE, GUYS! IF YOU'VE BEEN WALKING, LET'S PICK UP THE PACE, LET'S GO! LADIES! COME ON! LET'S GO!

SAVANNAH. I HAVE A CONDITION, MISTER!

FAHREN. *(She holds* **OSCAR** *for display.)* AND THIS GUY HAS A NOTE! AND A CONCUSSION!

>　　**(SONIA**, **ALYSSA**, **FAHREN**, *and* **MAURI** *trot for a bit, slowly, then return to walking.)*

My back hurts. You think I could have sciatica, too?

SAVANNAH. Probably. A lot of people do, I guess.

Ugh. I'm so thirsty now.

ALYSSA. Coach never lets anybody get water. Unless you go to the nurse / or something.

MAURI. Just tell him your stomach hurts.

FAHREN. Tell him you got cramps! He'll let you go.

SAVANNAH. I don't have cramps, / though.

MAURI. Just act like you do. He'll let you go, / I bet –

SAVANNAH. *(She tries it out.)* "Uggghhhh. Mister. I got cramps really bad. Could I go / to the –"

FAHREN. Nah, you gotta sound worse. Like, you gotta look like it actually hurts.

SAVANNAH. What do you mean? Like, what? Like –

>　　*(She tries again.)*

Like,

"Pleeeease mister. Uggghuh ooof it hurts so much. Ahhh!"

ALYSSA. That's pretty good. That's better.

It just needs to be more realistic. Here.

ALYSSA. Let me hit you.

SAVANNAH. NO! What the hell? / No!

SONIA. Don't hit her!

MAURI. *(He looks back.)* Oh shit. They're coming.

SONIA. Who?

> *(**LUIS**, **DAVID**, and **ERIC** almost run past the **GIRLS**. Then **FAHREN** steps in the way, and **SAVANNAH** joins her. **SONIA** does, too. **ALYSSA** hangs back with **MAURI** and **OSCAR**.)*

LUIS. Could you guys move?

FAHREN. Could you guys not be assholes?

LUIS. What?

SAVANNAH. You heard her. What she said. Gay rights!

DAVID. What are you guys / talking about?

FAHREN. You think that's cool to pick on your cousin like that, Eric?

Just cuz he's gay! / Just cuz he likes David!

OSCAR. Hey, maybe, is it cool, if you don't, like, yell it / and stuff?

FAHREN. *(To **OSCAR**.)* Oh, my bad. Not I didn't mean it in like, a bad way.

ERIC. We're not doing anything to him! Get out of the way, / Fahren!

FAHREN. Ey, culero! You hear me! You leave – What's your name?

MAURI. Oscar, his / name is Oscar.

FAHREN. YEAH! You better leave Oscar alone. You think that's fun? / To treat him –

LUIS. MOVE, FAHREN! WE GOTTA GO!

SAVANNAH. *(She pulls her hair back.)* Move or what? What are you gonna do if we don't?

What are you gonna do?

FAHREN. Yeah, what are you gonna do, huh? You gonna hit us?

You gonna give ME a concussion? Huh? / You wanna go?

SONIA. *(To* **FAHREN.***)* I think he gets it. We should go, guys. He's not / gonna –

FAHREN. Nah. We don't run.

LUIS. We didn't give him a concussion. He / fell! Move!

ERIC. We weren't picking on him. We're just trying to run. He's a liar, anyway.

MAURI. You kept trying to chase after him to make him fall, this / whole time.

ERIC. Nobody's talking to you, / bitch.

No, we weren't, we're just running.

SAVANNAH. Oh, hell no, who're you cussing at?

Nah, you don't know me, dude. / I'm crazy.

DAVID. Guys, let's go! Coach is gonna get / mad!

ALYSSA. I didn't think you'd be like that. Just cuz he liked you. Like, that's so messed up. You know my cousin's gay? Dick. Like, that's my favorite cousin. / I really thought –

DAVID. What does that have to do with anything?! I don't even know this freak.

Guys. Let's. Go.

SAVANNAH. Don't be calling him a freak! He's gay! It's normal!

LUIS. MOVE, GORDA!

> (**SAVANNAH** *sees red. She's activated.* **FAHREN**
> *feels her, too. Time moves slowest slow. Claude*
> *Debussy's "Clair de Lune."* **LUIS** *starts to run*
> *at* **SAVANNAH**, *but she drops him with her*
> *backpack.* **LUIS** *reaches for* **SAVANNAH**'s *bag,*
> *so she kicks his hand. She's an impressive*
> *opponent.* **LUIS** *screams.* **DAVID** *goes to pick*
> *up* **LUIS**, *so* **ALYSSA** *jumps him.*)

> (*Then,* **OSCAR** *steps outside of the scene. He's*
> *thirty now. He's much older. The mayhem*
> *continues in the background.*)

OSCAR. It was the first time I watched girls fight. I was
dazzled.

> (**SONIA** *steps out of time with* **OSCAR**. *She's*
> *older again now, too. They recognize each*
> *other, in this suspended future.*)

SONIA. Years from this point, I'll laugh about this. About
how much they didn't care.

> (**ALYSSA** *has jumped up on* **DAVID**, *scratching*
> *him. It's breathtaking; a dance.* **SAVANNAH**
> *is laughing at them.* **ERIC** *runs to get* **ALYSSA**
> *off of* **DAVID**. **MAURI** *launches himself against*
> **ERIC**, *tackling him.* **MAURI** *is impressed with*
> *himself; a triumph!* **ERIC** *falls to the ground,*
> *slow, like a Titan.*)

OSCAR. I'll miss them. How much they cared for me.
I don't think I would have survived that year without
them. I don't know how I would have survived high
school, either. I can't imagine it.

SONIA. I spent the rest of that school year helping Fahren
with her schoolwork. Picked up every time Alyssa

FaceTimed me to tell me about whoever she'd broken up with that month. Savannah's the first person I told when I got pregnant. Then, when I wasn't.

> (**ALYSSA** *gets* **DAVID** *to the ground, so he crawls to* **LUIS**, *who is agonizing.* **FAHREN** *runs to* **DAVID** *as he crawls; she climbs on his back, pulls his hair back, points to* **OSCAR** *and mouths "Leave him alone!")*

OSCAR. "Leave him alone!"

I can still hear her. Fahren. She had this raspy voice.

She always smelled like cigarettes and Victoria's Secret Love Spell.

I saw her and her mom share a pack of cigarettes at the bus stop once. I thought that was so cool.

> (**ERIC** *tries to get up, so* **MAURI** *knocks him, palms right on the bridge of his nose. Like a shark.* **SAVANNAH** *laughs and laughs. She reaches into her bag and pulls out a bag of Flamin' Hots.* Silently, she mouths, "Damn, that's crazy!")*

SONIA. "Damn, that's crazy!"

She would say that about everything. When she was listening to anything you'd tell her.

When she wasn't. "Damn, that's crazy."

She said it then, too, that day.

I was so scared we'd get in trouble that I just froze up. And I remember looking at Savannah, watching how much fun she was having with this mess.

I wanted to be her.

---

* A license to produce *Milewalkers* does not include a license to publicly display any branded logos or trademarked images. Licensees must acquire rights for any logos and/or images or create their own.

*(**DAVID** finally crawls to **LUIS** and tries to pick him back up. He can't. **LUIS** can't get up. His ankle hurts too much. He falls into **DAVID**'s arms. A Pietà. **ALYSSA** tries to charge at **DAVID** again, but **FAHREN** holds her back. The **BOYS** scream for Coach. **SAVANNAH** runs to the **GIRLS**. She feeds **ALYSSA** some Flamin' Hots to calm her down, like one would tend to a boxer. Tender. A middle-school boy Pietà, a middle-school girl Rembrandt.)*

OSCAR. After, Alyssa said "Don't let anybody pick on you like that again.

Seriously. If anybody fucks with you, you tell us. Or we'll beat you up."

When she said that, I believed her. Really. In a way, I don't think I've ever believed anybody else. Like, not even my parents.

After that, I told them everything.

*(**ERIC** holds his nose and tries to swipe at **MAURI** who is much quicker. With great effort, **ERIC** gets up and starts to move towards **LUIS** and **DAVID**. **ALYSSA** sees him, grabs some dirt from the ground and throws it in his face. **MAURI** moves behind him and pulls his shorts up into a wedgie; a painful one. **ERIC** falls once again. **ALYSSA** yells at him on the ground – "That's your cousin, pendejo!")*

SONIA. "That's your cousin, pendejo! That's your cousin!"

I think that's what pissed Alyssa off the most, is that Eric would do that to his own cousin.

Or maybe she just wanted to be mad at somebody.

I remember in college, I had this really awful breakup.

I didn't want therapy. I didn't want to be the bigger person.

I wanted to fight this guy. So bad.

I wished Alyssa had been around to beat the shit out of this guy.

She would have. Fahren, too.

Maybe not Savannah. She just liked to start shit. But she woulda brought snacks.

> (**ERIC** *crawls to* **LUIS** *and* **DAVID**. **ALYSSA**, **FAHREN**, **SAVANNAH**, *and* **MAURI** *are eating Flamin' Hots. Triumphant demons. The* **BOYS** *look terrified. The* **GIRLS** *are massive and lit like judgement. Slowly, the* **BOYS** *rise,* **DAVID** *and* **ERIC** *lifting* **LUIS** *up.*)

OSCAR. We fell out of touch eventually. Moved. Graduated. Moved again. Got busy. Followed each other on Instagram. Blocked each other on Twitter. Disappeared.

SONIA. Time does that, I guess. With enough time, people do that to each other. There's nothing extraordinary about this. But they felt that way. They felt absolutely extraordinary. Powerful.

OSCAR. Like they'd been born fully themselves.

SONIA. So entirely themselves. Deities. Furies.

OSCAR. I think about this moment a lot. Sometimes once a month, once a week, when I see a group of girls whispering secrets at the bus stop.

SONIA. Sometimes suddenly when I smell Marlboro Lights and body spray.

OSCAR. I get pulled right back here. Where I learned to let myself be protected.

SONIA. Right back here, where I learned to fight back and love it.

> (**DAVID** *and* **ERIC** *carry* **LUIS** *off.* **COACH DUARTE** *blows his whistle.* **OSCAR** *and* **SONIA** *get pulled back there again, all those years ago.*)

COACH DUARTE. HEY!!! WHAT THE HELL ARE YOU GUYS DOING!? GIRLS! LADIES!!!!

ALYSSA. Oh, shit.

FAHREN. *(She thinks.)* Run!

> (**COACH DUARTE** *blows his whistle over and over.* **OSCAR**, **SONIA**, **SAVANNAH**, **MAURI**, **FAHREN**, *and* **ALYSSA** *run, all those years ago. They run.)*

End of Play